PAPER GARDENS

PAPER GARDENS

A Stroll through French Literature

ÉVELYNE BLOCH-DANO

Translated by Teresa Lavender Fagan

University of Virginia Press · Charlottesville and London

Publication of this translation was assisted by a grant from the French Ministry of Culture, Centre national du livre.

This work received the French Voices Award for excellence in publication and translation. French Voices is a program created and funded by the French Embassy in the United States and FACE (French American Cultural Exchange). (French Voices Logo designed by Serge Bloch)

Originally published in French as *Jardins de papier: De Rousseau à Modiano*
© Éditions Stock, 2015

University of Virginia Press
Printed in the United States of America on acid-free paper

First published 2018
1 3 5 7 9 8 6 4 2

Library of Congress Cataloging-in-Publication Data

Names: Bloch-Dano, Évelyne, author. | Fagan, Teresa Lavender, translator.
Title: Paper gardens : a stroll through French literature / Évelyne Bloch-Dano ; Translated by Teresa Lavender Fagan.
Other titles: Jardins de papier. English
Description: Charlottesville ; London : University of Virginia Press, 2018. | Originally published in French as Jardins de papier: De Rousseau à Modiano. | Includes bibliographical references.
Identifiers: LCCN 2017048409 | ISBN 9780813940250 (hardcover : alk. paper) | ISBN 9780813940274 (e-book)
Subjects: LCSH: French literature—Themes, motives. | Gardens in literature. | Gardens—Symbolic aspects.
Classification: LCC PQ145.1.G345 B5613 2018 | DDC 840.9/364—dc23
LC record available at https://lccn.loc.gov/2017048409
Cover art: Peony from nineteenth-century illustration (Dover Publications); *Recherche du temps perdu* proofs hand-marked by Marcel Proust, 1913 (The Rare Book & Manuscript Library, University of Illinois at Urbana-Champaign)

TO PIERRE

I've dreamed of a book you can open
the way you push open the door of an
abandoned garden.

—Christian Bobin

CONTENTS

FOREWORD

In more than ten books, to the delight of a large and loyal French readership, Évelyne Bloch-Dano has reinvented the art of biography. Each of her books offers a new angle on a subject we thought we knew, illuminating obliquely, rather than head-on.

She began her life's work by shifting her gaze from the great men of the literary pantheon to the extraordinary yet unsung women in their lives: Madame Zola—Émile Zola's wife; the messianic Flora Tristan; and my own favorite, Jeanne Weil Proust, Marcel Proust's mother. Her novel set in postwar France, *La Biographe* [The biographer], is a meditation on the relationship of a biographer to her subject—a connection she explores in each of her books.

For fifteen years, Évelyne Bloch-Dano wrote about writers' homes, and these articles—small masterpieces of descriptive prose—have been gathered into a book called *Mes Maisons d'écrivains* [My writers' houses]. Every time I open her *Madame Proust*, I find myself in the Prousts' heavily draperied Paris apartment, where Marcel is translating Ruskin under his mother's watchful eye, acquiring the discipline he will muster to complete *In Search of Lost Time.* It's only a short step from these domestic spaces to the backyards of Colette and Sand that she so vividly renders here. Most recently, Bloch-Dano has written the story of the Proust "questionnaire," introducing us for the first time to the forgotten circle of Proust's young friends who engaged with him in that famous parlor game.

Two of her books—I think of these as Bloch-Dano's "eco-biographies"—stand out as biographies not just of people but of the world of living things. The first is her 2012 *Vegetables: A Biography.* Here she tracks the life stories of carrots, cabbage, pumpkins, peas, on plates and in poetry, restoring to our senses the true taste of these foods and offering both ancient history and modern recipes. We learn about the inspirational qualities of parsnips from Samuel Beckett, and about the virtues of artichokes from Sigmund Freud.

Now in *Paper Gardens,* Bloch-Dano ushers us through the garden gates of France's greatest writers. Not only does she enable us to read these authors differently, through the attention they give in their writing to plants and parks and orchards, she also enables us to understand gardens differently than we might otherwise. A garden, Bloch-Dano shows us, is not just a collection of flowers and herbs. A garden exists both in nature and in language; it bears the traces of civilization, of taste, of culture, every bit as much as literature itself.

All to say that these "paper gardens" signify "garden" in the largest sense of the word: the public garden, so formative of children's lives in Paris; the family garden of the French provinces; the secret garden and the lost gardens of our dreams. Gardens we have weeded, cultivated, fertilized, or, just as powerfully, the gardens we have imagined. Her writers cultivate gardens in their fiction, or, like Colette, they dream of the gardens of their childhood. She even takes on Jean-Paul Sartre outdoors, showing his phobic relationship with nature, the invasive vegetation and rotten trees of his novels and stories and his recurrent dreams of heroic exploits in the Luxembourg Gardens. Her chapter on Patrick Modiano captures the ghostly scent of public gardens in the dark: "We were floating in a night perfumed by the privet shrub on the fence when we passed in front of the Parc Monceau."

Paper Gardens is a garden's-eye view of the history of French literature and an invitation, since all of the writers she discusses here—from Rousseau, Sand, and Balzac to Proust, Gide, Colette, and many others—are part of an American literary heritage through the canon of translated works. We, her American readers, can delight in bringing Évelyne Bloch-Dano's vision home to our own writers' gardens, reading them as she might. Edith Wharton created the vast landscapes at The Mount, which stand today, along with her fiction, as an embodiment of her achievements. Thomas Jefferson's south-facing vegetable garden at Monticello was a scientific experiment worthy of the French Enlightenment. Thoreau designed a kitchen garden for Hawthorne as a wedding present. And who can forget one of Évelyne Bloch-Dano's favorite American writers, Louisa May Alcott, whose portraits in *Little Women* define the March girls through their individual garden plots: "Meg's had roses and heliotrope, myrtle, and a little orange tree in it. Jo's bed was never alike two seasons, for she was always trying experiments. . . . Beth had old-fashioned fragrant flowers in her garden, sweet peas and mignonette, larkspur, pinks, pansies, and southernwood, with chickweed for the birds and catnip for the pussies.

Amy had a bower in hers, rather small and earwiggy, but very pretty to look at, with honeysuckle and morning-glories hanging their colored horns and bells in graceful wreaths all over it, tall white lilies, delicate ferns, and as many brilliant, picturesque plants as would consent to blossom there."

In her introduction to *Paper Gardens,* Bloch-Dano invites her readers to wander through her book as they might stroll through a park, stopping with one writer or another to pick a blossom or watch a tree sway in the wind, turning a corner from Henri IV's Tuileries to the estate of Simone de Beauvoir's grandfather at Meyrignac. This is a book to savor in no particular order, or to read from start to finish as a literary history; to enjoy in moments of leisure, ten minutes at a time, or to dive into for happy hours of contemplation.

Reading *Paper Gardens* is bound to have a powerful effect on your imagination; indeed it is guaranteed to conjure the favorite gardens of your own past. For me it was Hans Christian Andersen's Little Mermaid in her underwater garden, and closer to home, my mother's rock garden and the hedge of thick white peonies separating our lawn from the neighbors'. As I was reading her chapter on Marguerite Duras, for no discernible reason, I remembered the day my friend Connie and I discovered a Japanese gingko tree in the rose garden off Lake Harriet Boulevard. Among the gifts that Évelyne Bloch-Dano offers her readers in this magical book is to make us all into authors of our own gardens.

Alice Kaplan

PAPER GARDENS

"I WENT DOWN TO MY GARDEN . . ."

What I find so tiresome about the sea is that there
are no flowers in it. Imagine fields of hollyhocks
and violets in mid-ocean! How divine!

—Virginia Woolf, *The Voyage Out*

The buzzing of a fly, the beating of a butterfly's wings, the
smell of damp earth, the transparent air pierced by a swallow,
the sound of a rooster in the distance, the dance of a butterfly
above the lavender, the scurrying of bees above the fennel, the
scent of freshly cut grass, the rustling of leaves, the flight of a
lizard: a garden is a world of sounds, movement, scents—wisteria, roses, honeysuckle, mint, thyme, strawberries—life in a
concentrated form. And all those visible and invisible creatures
underground, in the air, spiders nestled in the corner of a window, strolling flies, tawny owls in the night, warblers in the
shrubs, moles on the hunt, ants in a hurry, languid slugs, singing frogs, skittering lizards, and all those insects whose names
I don't know . . . They are all a part of it, feed it and feed from
it, animate it, make it live. And why not the cows in the adjoining field that graze dreamily, since their powerful odor joins
in waves that of the plants? The architecture of my garden in
Normandy is traditional, the work of the previous owner, the

village mailman: an orchard below a meadow, vegetables growing on the left, flowers on the right, opposite the house. In the
yard there are lilacs and a willow tree, along the edges a riot of
perennials—peonies, daisies, phlox, geraniums—and a fig tree
that freezes in the winter and is reborn each spring. None of
this can be seen from the little road that leads to the forest. It
is not one of those gardens that shouts for attention, but it isn't
shy, either. Nor is my other garden, in Île-de-France, a grassy
square of land with clay soil where roses, asters and, yes, hydrangeas in their September purple splendor are at home.
A vine purchased at a market in Provence runs along the terrace, collapsing under the weight of the muscat grapes like the
plum tree under its fruit. The cherry tree is showing its age, the
stalks of white corn that we planted last spring seem sad, but
the witch hazel looks promising.

I haven't always had gardens. But what does it mean to
"have" a garden? For years I enjoyed the gardens of others: vacation rentals, country homes of my school friends, or parks
filled with the fragrance of lilacs which we would stroll around
with my father, wanting them for ourselves . . . We lived in
a fifth-floor apartment and, like all children in Paris, my first
gardens were public: the dusty square at the Porte de Cham-
perret or, sometimes, the lavish Parc Monceau. There was
the little garden of my grandparents in Lorraine where, when
I was three, with my dog Bouboule, I would escape the watchful eyes of the adults and sit amid the cabbages and munch on
curly parsley. Because the pleasure of a garden is also solitude.
Freedom in a protected place. A bubble in the ongoing march
of time.

My father, who left his village in Alsace for Paris when he was young, liked both the city and nature. He sought out the noise, the animation, the cars, the movie theaters, the crowd. But he had a very strong yearning and a need, I believe, for the land. My parents, who were not well-off, later in life were able to purchase a small country house in the Oise. The vegetable garden never went beyond a few stalks of tarragon, parsley, and thyme, currant and raspberry bushes, cuttings from which still bear fruit in my increasingly cramped and late-blooming Île-de-France garden. They, too, are beginning to age . . . My father's passion was flowers. We would go to pick them in the woods around Paris, the first violets, wild hyacinth, lily of the valley; he would gather them in bouquets held together by a blade of grass. We uncovered mauve-colored lilacs and I would plunge my face into their heady fragrance. He would give my mother flowers for any occasion. Nothing made him prouder than those that he sowed, planted, and cared for in his garden in the Oise.

But when I was a child, my parents rented a house in Seine-et-Marne for the month of July. My father would join us in the evenings. Between the ages of ten and fifteen, I invented there my own way of experiencing gardens. It hasn't really changed. I helped him plant the flowers, water the rose bushes carefully, pick off the yellowed leaves of the geraniums. I watched him mow the meadow behind the house. I would push the wheelbarrow. I played a useful role, was the admiring witness to his efforts. I don't have a very green thumb, I must admit. It's not for lack of trying, though. But the results are often mediocre. I lack application and perseverance in this realm. My role is

3

limited most of the time to designing the garden, choosing and arranging the plants, maintaining the edges of the flower beds, weeding, cutting wilted roses, picking green beans, lettuce, squash . . .

In Boissise-la-Bertrand I would dream, I would spend hours reading under the arbor or on the swing that my father hung from the branch of an apple tree—a simple wooden plank suspended by ropes which he took down at the end of the vacation and put up again the following year. I would write in my diary while listening to "Salut les copains" on the patio edged with lavender, behind the house.

As soon as we arrived at the house we would pick the lock on the glass-doored bookcase where there were dozens of novels in the Nelson collection. Dumas, Balzac, Chateaubriand, I read them, devoured them, those summers, in the garden. The Countess of Charny, the knight of Maison-Rouge, Eugénie Grandet, Atala, and so many others inhabited the garden footpaths and the yard. Later, my reading material, then dictated by my teachers, was filled with tormented heroines: Thérèse Desqueyroux, Emma Bovary, Gervaise, Madame de Rénal, and, my favorite, Natasha Rostov, with whom I passionately identified . . . I no longer saw the garden, but I felt it around me. It vibrated. It took me in its arms. I reveled in the calm, the space unfolding before me, the slight vertigo when I would raise my head to follow a fly on my glass of milk or a butterfly flying off. Emma basking on a chaise longue, Natasha arranging daisies in her hair. Except I was the only one to see them.

And so it is understandable that gardens and reading are inseparable for me. My choice of writers for this book is personal, subjective, limited to France, I must point out. I would have liked to have summoned the memory of Karen Blixen, of Edith Wharton, or of Vita Sackville-West. Vita above all, whose gardens at Sissinghurst—the famous White Garden, among others—reveal a true passion and a know-how shared with her husband, Harold Nicholson, abilities far superior to those of most writers. For years she wrote a column in the *Observer* offering enlightened, humorous advice such as: "The true gardener must be brutal, and imaginative for the future." I love referring to her writing like an almanac, and nothing is more delightful than those addresses for English nurseries, most of which have disappeared.

And so I have limited myself to French novelists, choosing great prose writers whose gardens make up an essential element of their work. Of course, gardens are already found in courtly and precious literature, such as the "garden of flowers" at the edge of a forest, seen from the pavilion where the duc de Nemours watches the confession of Madame de Clèves to her husband, then, through the lighted window, the beauty contemplating the duke's image while tying ribbons around a cane . . . On the one side, the raked footpaths of the grounds where the Princesse strolls with her husband, on the other, the flower garden surrounded by hedges and a fairy-tale forest, obscure places of desire . . .

Why do I begin with Jean-Jacques Rousseau? Because he was the first in French literature to turn the garden into a refuge and the mirror of intimate feelings. From Les Charmettes of Madame de Warens to the Elysium of Julie, he wove together idealized memories and a fictionalized ideal. Chateaubriand's

5

Mémoires d'outre-tombe opens with a passionate evocation of his park of Châtenay. About the trees planted as souvenirs of his travels, he writes: "They are my family, I have no other, I hope to die in their midst." A large number of nineteenth-century writers follow Rousseau, beginning with George Sand, of course, and those love scenes in the garden echoing Stendhal and Flaubert, Balzac, Hugo and Zola. For the first half of the twentieth century, there was Marcel Proust, André Gide, Colette, Simone de Beauvoir, and, paradoxically, Jean-Paul Sartre, the man who hated trees. The choice is more difficult when we get closer to the present day: Marguerite Duras, Patrick Modiano, and Christian Bobin. Their gardens are rooted in the imaginary, are fed on their dreams, their memories, they spread out in a fantasized or poetic space often connected to childhood.

I introduce these garden studies by taking the reader on a rapid journey into the history of gardens, to discover their origins and diversity. Building a bridge between real gardens and imaginary gardens enables them to be mutually understood. For this, it's impossible to stay just in France, so numerous are the influences from around the world. The humus is enriched by contributions from lands distant in time and space. I have looked at only a few of them, the most remarkable in my opinion. The founding text of our culture is, of course, the story of the Garden of Eden in the Bible. Interpretations of that story are inexhaustible. Our concept of gardens comes out of it. Intimately linked to events, conquests, art, culture, science, sensibility, sociology, anthropology, technology, symbolism, myths, and to the history of taste and aesthetics, gardens are the reflection of societies and individuals. But they also tell us a lot about those who contemplate them: today we don't look at a French-style garden as they did in the nineteenth century, for example. And what about the painters! Every garden, however modest it may be, tells us about the dreams, the ideal of happiness, the utopia of the one who created it and described it, as well as about the society that produced it. A garden is a vector of the imaginary, and it is also for that reason that gardens play a special role in novels.

Remember the books by the Comtesse de Ségur . . . The gardens of the perfect little girls were both a pedagogical tool and a territory of freedom. How I dreamed of them when I was a child! Through those gardens, Camille and Madeleine learned about responsibility, developed a sense of ownership, a taste for work well done, and the pleasure of tasting and sharing. In the big park of *Les Vacances,* they constructed huts with their cousins, they chased each other, they had picnics on the grass, they played, they hid. A garden enables the carefree life of childhood and teaches valuable lessons for adulthood. Under the authority of a ferociously Rousseauian mother, Sophie de Ségur drew on the teachings of her own youth on the huge estate of the Rostopchines near Moscow and the Château des Nouettes in the Orne, then drew on the bitter fruits of her migraine-filled life as a deceived wife. Her salvation was later in writing for her grandchildren, who visited her on her estate.

If some of the writers I present were true gardeners, happy to wield the spade or the dibble, like George Sand, André Gide, or to a lesser degree, Colette, others, such as Marcel Proust or Honoré de Balzac, had no experience with gardening. Some were enthralled with botany, such as Jean-Jacques Rousseau, George Sand, or André Gide; for the city dwellers Jean-Paul Sartre or Patrick Modiano, it was the public garden that was a source of inspiration.

All of them turned their gardens of words, derived—or not—from real life, into a microcosm of their work and their style. That enclosed space, often evoked as the continuation of a house, both inside and out, is placed within the mental landscape that opens up around it. A simple descriptive setting, or intimately connected to the profound meaning of the text and its dynamics, the garden reveals the imaginary of the writer, and the specific form of his or her art. As in a Japanese garden, it is the very essence of the writer's universe that is then exhaled from the pages when we turn them.

Stroll freely through this book as you would through a park. Follow a path, maybe skip one, stop, retrace your steps, breathe in the scent of a metaphor or wander around a detour of a phrase in your own memory. And above all, cultivate your own garden, right in the ground, in pots, in dreams, or in words . . .

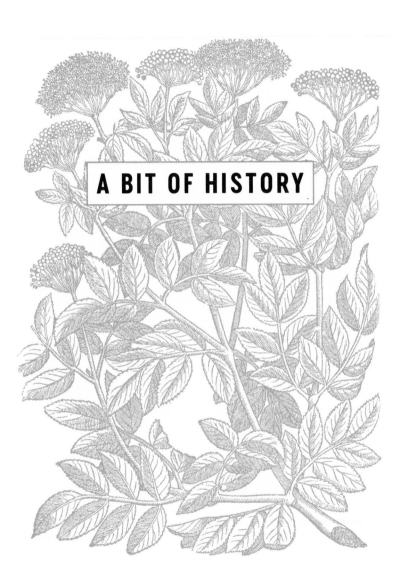

A BIT OF HISTORY

Words from the Garden

The French word *jardin*—garden—comes from the Frankish *gart,* which designates an enclosed piece of land. This root is found in the German *garten* and the English *garden.*

❀

In the Middle Ages one spoke of the *clos,* a cultivated plot enclosed by walls or shrubbery, or of the *courtil* (from the Latin *curtis*), an enclosed garden, often of modest size, adjoining a farm.

❀

Parc—park, or grounds—comes from the Low Latin *parricus,* "enclosure." It designates a vast expanse of enclosed land and woods where animals that were raised for hunting were kept.

❀

Verger—orchard—(from the Latin *viridarium,* from *viridis,* "green") designates a place planted with fruit trees. In the Middle Ages it was the common term used to designate both a pleasure (flower) garden and a garden planted with fruit trees.

❀

Jardin became widespread beginning in the second half of the thirteenth century, first replacing *ort* (*hortillon*), from the Latin *hortus* and designating a vegetable garden.

To describe the garden of Déduit in the *Roman de la Rose,* Guillaume de Lorris often uses *vergier* and quite rarely *jardin* (only for the rhyme), whereas his continuator, Jean de Meung, uses *jardin* more frequently than *vergier* (only once for the rhyme). The two terms competed with each other until the end of the fifteenth century.

(Source: Centre national de ressources textuelles et lexicales)

Paradis—paradise—from the Median *pairi daeza* (royal estate), turned into the Persian *pardès* to designate any planted and enclosed garden, then into the Greek *paradeisos* to designate the enclosed parks of Persian rulers where wild animals were kept.

GARDENS OF ORIGINS

Life begins the day one plants a garden.

—Chinese proverb

The first garden, at the dawn of humanity, was composed of a few plants protected from the wind, the sand, and animals by an enclosure made of thorny bushes. The hunter-gatherers had not disappeared, the nomadic peoples moved their herds following the seasons, sedentism was just getting under way. There were probably a handful of individuals or a few groups who stopped for a bit longer and discovered—to their surprise—that the seeds or the plants they had put in the ground were growing, becoming green, and in turn were providing seeds, fruit, and leaves that could be eaten. Imagine the delight of the man who for the first time was able to feed his family with the fruit of his labor on that morning when he saw a little sprout sticking up out of the ground, a flowering bud on a tree that he had planted with his own hands. His wonderment. How glorious he must have found all that. And so he wanted to protect his garden, settle down and stay put long enough to see the bounty of mother earth grow and multiply. He carefully extracted the weeds so that his plants could enjoy the water he poured over them with care and love. How greatly he must have feared the sun that scorches, the rain that floods, and the cold that withers.

The first garden provided food, but it was also a source of pleasure, because every gardener admires what he or she produces, the shade of the trees he or she has planted, the buds that tell of fruit to come. I believe that what was useful and what was pleasurable blossomed together on that first day. Yes, the first garden was an Eden: a garden of delights. A paradise.

Gardens have retained a trace of that miracle and have for a long time been associated with myths of origins and fertility. But they are essentially ephemeral, and we will never know the shapes or the exact colors of the first garden, or those that followed it. We can only guess, deduce, imagine. Gardens carry within them the eternal cycle of the seasons, but they can be transformed and often disappear. They are the reflections of the civilizations that produced them, and they can die out with those civilizations. They flourished over the entire earth, but the scent of their flowers reaches us only through writing and illustrations.

In the heart of the Fertile Crescent, on the banks of the Persian Gulf (present-day Iraq), on the plains irrigated by the Tigris and the Euphrates, more than three thousand years before the Christian era, the Sumerians left the first written traces of a garden in a tale about Enki, the god of fertility. Enki, the gardener, offers an abundance of giant apples, cucumbers, and grapes to the beautiful Uttu, whom he then seduces and "floods with his seed": fertility of the earth and fecundity of the woman go hand in hand, they are indistinguishable. Man assumes the role of gardener-creator. The garden is inscribed in founding myths, it is associated with the cult of the divinities, its sacred value associates it with temples, with tales of origins. From the biblical Eden to the funerary gardens of ancient Egypt, from the Roman woods to the paradise promised by Allah, the supreme gardener, gardens are found in most Western religions both as parables and as metaphors. "The God of the Bible is the great gardener who separates the land and the sea, makes plants grow, and causes man and woman to be born, but he assigns Adam the task of naming." Gardens, like the biblical story, are the creations of men.

The Bible story of the creation of the world shows a marked Mesopotamian influence. But the Hebrew language and Jewish culture give it its unique flavor and meaning, which are subject to countless interpretations. Unlike other cosmogonies, the Bible introduces a single God, abstract, transcendent. The Greek translation of the Septuagint turned the Garden of Eden into "paradise." But the Hebrew *pardès* (from the Persian), which means "grove," is used only three times in the Old Testament (*Song of Solomon, Ecclesiastes,* and *Nehemiah*). From a garden in Eden, the text moves to the Garden of Eden. The Hebrew expression *gan eden*—"garden of delights"—stresses the dual component of the garden: security (*gan* comes from a verb that means "to protect") and enjoyment (*eden*). Does this mean that the one must always accompany the other? The first task assigned to man in the Bible story is that of gardener. If Adam, the man made of clay (from *adama,* "earth"), is put in the garden, it is so he will take care of the divine creation. As for the tree of the knowledge of good and evil, our tradition, by way of the Latin translation (*malum,* "round fruit"), associates it with the apple tree. In truth, we don't know anything about the plants that grew in that garden; the emphasis is placed only on the two symbolic trees at its center.

Man wasn't forbidden pleasure; on the contrary. Adam could eat freely of all the fruit of the garden, including that of the tree of life that would ensure he would live forever. But that divine permission was accompanied by an interdict: that of eating the fruit of "the tree of the knowledge of good and evil." Permission and interdict are the two sides of the Law that the Bible text places in the center of the Garden of Eden. And the interdict does indeed deal with morality, and not with knowledge in general, as is sometimes claimed. The Law places limits on the satisfaction of desires. Adam and Eve's "crime" was perhaps that they were unable to be content with what the Garden offered them . . . How many are denied paradise out of an excess of greed and cupidity?

Adam is initially in the *gan eden* in a childlike state. He is alone, Eve hasn't yet been created. He is on this side of moral awareness, and the only rule he must follow is to obey his Creator. What he is permitted is "good," and what he is forbidden is "evil." Later, Adam's and Eve's eyes would be opened only through their transgression. To eat the fruit of the tree of the knowledge of good and evil was to attempt to be God's equal. The Hebrew word used for knowledge (*da'at*) has the same root as the verb that means "to know" in the biblical sense, indeed, it is a carnal, intimate, deep knowledge. It means to experience

The Garden of Eden

And the LORD God planted a garden eastward in Eden; and there he put the man whom he had formed. And out of the ground made the LORD God to grow every tree that is pleasant to the sight, and good for food; the tree of life also in the midst of the garden, and the tree of knowledge of good and evil.

And a river went out of Eden to water the garden; and from thence it was parted, and became into four heads. The name of the first is Pison: that is it which compasseth the whole land of Havilah, where there is gold; And the gold of that land is good: there is bdellium and the onyx stone. And the name of the second river is Gihon: the same is it that compasseth the whole land of Ethiopia. And the name of the third river is Hiddekel: that is it which goeth toward the east of Assyria. And the fourth river is Euphrates.

And the LORD God took the man, and put him into the garden of Eden to dress it and to keep it. And the Lord God commanded the man, saying: "Of every tree of the garden thou mayest freely eat: But of the tree of the knowledge of good and evil, thou shalt not eat of it: for in the day that thou eatest thereof thou shalt surely die."

(Genesis 2:8-17, King James Version)

the complexity of morality, of the tangling of the notions of good and evil. Banished from the wonderful garden, Adam would have to ensure his survival by the sweat of his brow by farming an unproductive land, and Eve, to give birth in pain. They would discover a life of wandering, of work, of suffering and death: the finiteness of the human condition. The biblical myth reminds us that the human story can only begin beyond paradise.

The literary texts devoted to the garden retain a trace of that founding tale of our culture: the security of an enclosed space, enjoyment, but also, quite often, the Law and its transgression. No one remains in paradise. But all gardens maintain the memory of it . . .

The Genesis story situates the Garden of Eden in the same geographical zone as Sumer and Babylon, between the Tigris and the Euphrates, in the East where the sun rises. This is not by chance; it is probably in that region of the Fertile Crescent that the acclimation of the date palm created and maintained enough humidity to plant and cultivate zones of vegetation. The mention of the four rivers is important, as they are an additional factor of fertility in an arid region. Of course, nothing enables us to locate Eden precisely: it is a myth. But for a long time explorers have looked for it. Christopher Columbus thought he had found the garden, so the story goes, near the Orinoco River, and others have looked for it in India and China.

Historians agree that in the second millennium BC rulers in Mesopotamia liked to surround their palaces with gardens. Later, Assyrian kings would fill their vast estates with wild animals for hunting, would have irrigation canals dug to enable the planting of cedars, palm trees, and cypresses and to water their orchards filled with almond, pear, fig, apple, and pomegranate trees. For a long time, vegetable and pleasure gardens would similarly be inseparable.

Was it under Nebuchadnezzar II, as the Judean historian Flavius Josephus believed, that the famous Hanging Gardens of Babylon were constructed in the sixth century BC? Written sources differ, but the gardens' existence is no longer doubted. Babylon's ideal location at the narrowest point between the Tigris and the Euphrates favored irrigation, innovation, and commercial trade. The gardens were located near the Ishtar Gate, Ishtar being the goddess of fertility, outside the fortifications, overlooking the plains of the Euphrates. The terracing in increasingly narrow plots, the ingeniousness of watering techniques using waterfalls, the waves of flowering and bushy vegetation, fascinated those who saw the gardens and were inscribed in the memories of travelers, as well as in the collective imagination, making the Hanging Gardens of Babylon the seventh wonder of the world for the Greeks. The gardens combined architecture and natural elements, the myth of fertility and symbols of power, dreams and reality, all constants in the history of gardens.

> To see the gardens of Babylon,
> And the palace of the Great Lama
> To dream of lovers in Verona,
> At the top of Fujiyama,

sang Henri Salvador. How can one not dream while hearing about all these gardens, Sumerian, Babylonian, Egyptian, that plunge their roots into millennial history and bear witness to the ingeniousness of humans as they work to feed themselves and to adjust to the rhythm of the seasons, to the circulation of knowledge, and the aspiration for beauty? A garden, both the original vegetable garden and the landscaped park, is planned and unfolds around water. While the gardener uses water judiciously in his vegetable garden, in palace gardens it flows generously through fountains, it gushes forth, bubbles in pools, it is a symbol of profusion, of gratuitousness, and of wealth. But there can be no garden without a concerted mastery of nature, a close understanding of its features, its needs, and its whims. A garden reflects the profound nature of the one who creates or cultivates it and, beyond the gardener's personality, of the civilization that produced him or her. It is nature and culture, space and representation, production and utopia. It speaks to us of happiness. It speaks to us of us. A garden is a mirror.

Persian Gardens

The art of the Persian garden (*pardès* or "paradise") can be seen in the style of the *chahar bagh,* a rectangle of vegetation divided into four smaller rectangles laid out in the form of a cross. It is surrounded by irrigation canals fed by basins with four openings. Shaded, featuring small structures where one can find shelter from the sun, chat, or rest, soothed by the murmuring of the fountains and the chirping of birds, these paradisiac Persian gardens would give birth to the gardens of Islam in the Maghreb and Spain after inspiring the Greeks, then the Romans. But, above all, the *chahar bagh* of the Persian rulers turned the *pardès* into a symbol of power and order. Persian rugs offer a colorful and sublimated image of *pardès*. The motif of the *chahar bagh* appeared following the Mongol invasions, suggesting that these rugs were a way of preserving the memory of a devastated paradise. And it is said that they also enabled the Sassanid rulers in the sixth century BC to bring their gardens inside the walls of their palaces in the winter. But, above all, the rugs symbolically perpetuated the image of the world over which those rulers reigned. Rug gardens and garden rugs communicated between the interior and exterior worlds.

ROMAN GARDENS

Rome absorbed, synthesized, and interpreted the characteristics of the civilizations it encountered in the course of its conquests. This art of synthesis is found in the history of Rome's gardens, of the sacred woods where Romans venerated the divine forces of nature in the most elaborate forms of garden architecture.

A foundation of rusticity connected the Roman to his garden, his *hortus,* which produced cabbage (a favorite of Cato), squash, but also olive trees and grapevines as well as all the other vegetables and fruits destined for his consumption. His relationship to nature was inseparable from his religion. From the beginning, the lares gods, which preceded Priapus, then Venus, Pomona, and Flora, connected the garden to the home, to the house.

Greek influence would enlarge this conception, even if classical Greece wasn't very interested in gardens per se. Plato's Academy, Aristotle's Lyceum, the garden of Epicurus — they all associate gardens with philosophy. This influential notion was wielded primarily through literature: Homer — the fantastic garden of Calypso, or Ulysses's return to Ithaca, when he recognizes his father hiding in the clothes of a gardener — the Alexandrine poets or the Persian novels of Xenophon, describing oriental *pardès*. But it was above all the first gardens they encountered in Magna Graecia and in Sicily, then in the East, notably in Persia and Egypt, that would fascinate the Romans. Greek harmony, the grandiose nature and sense of symmetry of the Eastern paradises, enabled them to envision the aesthetic possibilities of a pleasure garden. They would be the first to separate that type of garden from vegetable gardens. Their belief in a sacralized nature and their own genius would endow the garden with a new dimension.

The techniques of the *topiarius* (the word is of Greek origin), a landscape artist, enabled Rome to make its mark on the art of gardens. In their work, those painters revealed a number of *topia*, both themes and symbols, which would be reinterpreted in gardens: the promontory, water, the sacred woods, the sanctuary . . . The close connection with painting, which was both a source of inspiration and a reflection (because it would in turn be influenced by gardens), was born in Rome. Thus one went from the life-giving *hortus* to landscape art.

Roman interest in gardens began in the second century BC, and vast estates, the *villae,* covered the right bank of the Tiber, the Pincio, and later, the land around the Vatican and the Esquiline Hill, creating a green belt around the city. The first large urban park we know of was that of the fabulously wealthy Lucullus, famous for his conquests in the East and for his love of gastronomy. His reputation reached its apogee around 60 BC, a date when eastern and Hellenistic influences could already be observed. Those huge gardens became symbols of political power in the image of the Porticus of Pompey or, later, Nero's Domus Aurea as described by Suetonius. The sacred wood (*lucus*), once wild, became aestheticized. Huge public parks, featuring borders of boxwood, decorated with porticoes or colonnades, baths prolonged with gardens and decorated with landscape frescoes, reveal the Roman taste for a synthesis between nature and artifice.

We know of Roman gardens above all from the accounts of writers such as Cicero in his letters to his friend Atticus, from whom he commissioned statues for his villa of Tusculum, or Pliny the Younger in his more detailed descriptions. The *villa* fulfilled both the desire for owning property and that for *otium* (leisure). Gardens were conducive to solitude, reflection, conversations with friends, but also, as at the time of the death of Cicero's daughter, to meditation in a sanctuary. The Roman attitude toward nature was modified, the horizon opened, but one sought less an expanse than a panorama. Virgil, Horace, and Ovid would in turn sing of the charms of the countryside in poems that were often inspired more by gardens than by untamed nature. Horace wrote:

> This was my prayer: a piece of land, not of great size,
> With a garden, and a permanent spring near the house,
> And above them a stretch of woodland. The gods gave
> More and better. It's fine. I ask for nothing else.
>
> (*Satires,* 2.6)

This *villa* landscape first appeared as an enlargement of the living space. The homes of rich landowners opened up onto the garden instead of facing inward around an atrium, a feature that gradually disappeared. Substituting for the earlier vegetable garden behind the house, the peristyle extended it.

But the garden also penetrated inside the house, by way of the interior decoration of the *topiarius,* who portrayed his realistic landscapes on the walls, as seen in the frescoes of Pompeii or those in the villa of Livia in Prima Porta. "Thus," concludes Pierre Grimal, "the garden, real, imaginary, or symbolic, was found everywhere in the décor as well as in the layout of the house." There was a variety of items placed within a garden that had different characteristics: copse, clearing, sanctuary, basin, grotto, and so forth. Parks became true microcosms, such as the Tivoli gardens in which the emperor Hadrian wanted to assemble prestigious architectural styles from around the world.

Nature was not, however, absent from them. There were few flowers, but greenery abounded in the space: there were plane trees and cypresses, garlands of climbing plants and shrubs (ivy, bay, myrtle, acanthus, oleanders). Aviaries (for peacocks and doves) and game parks reflected an eastern influence. Water flowed in canals, burst out of fountains, filled basins and pools. Sacred grottoes, tombs, statues, and sculpted shrubs evoking legendary scenes were reminders that the Gods were never far from the gardens.

This informed art, full of symbols, combining nature and architecture, painting and landscape, religion and Epicureanism, was to have a profound influence on the history of Western gardens.

MEDIEVAL GARDENS

For the most part, historians maintain that the art of the garden began in the Renaissance. And so the great pleasure gardens, which were often the results of architectural, even theoretical, research, are highlighted. But, of course, there was an abundance of gardens before that period, more modest perhaps, but just as important: vegetable gardens, gardens for medicinal plants intended for the herbalist's shop, bourgeois gardens or gardens of the nobility, and monastery gardens. Each in its own way, they speak of the domestic, religious, literary, or symbolic space of their time. Books of hours, miniatures, and paintings enable us to imagine those gardens with their tall walls, their geometric plantings, and their fountains placed in the center of everything.

The vegetable garden, inseparable from the house, was often rented with the living quarters. The lease sometimes specified what the garden was to contain, with, in some regions, cabbage occupying half the surface, leaving the rest to leeks, beets, onions, and beans. Those sustenance gardens were well named: they were indispensable, and the year followed the rhythm of seasonal crops that enabled growers to put vegetables in the "pot." Peas, dried beans and legumes along with grains—all essential foods—assured one's survival. Since vegetables from the garden were not subject to a tithe, they escaped the rigor of the tax levy. In a society threatened by the cyclical return of food shortages, even famine, with a few fowl and rabbits, a hive, aromatic herbs, which were also used for their medicinal properties—thyme for digestion, hyssop for coughs, sage (*salvia* in Latin) for all illnesses—a few fruit trees and a vine for verjuice, the Ancien Régime peasant, as well as the artisan or the bourgeois in the city, was guaranteed survival. One must never forget the vegetable garden: it constituted the base, the foundation of the art of the garden. "Out of the vegetable garden are born all gardens; it traverses time and contains knowledge" (Gilles Clement, *Une brève histoire du jardin*).

Food plants appear in Charlemagne's foundational text, the capitulary *De Villis,* a series of measures aiming to organize the huge estates of his empire. Among the articles (*capitula*), three concern agriculture and provide a precise idea of the plants that were grown in the gardens, since more than a hundred are listed: "greens" such as chard, chicory, watercress, orache, lettuce, marigold or mallow, and cabbage; root vegetables such as Umbellifers: carrots, parsnips or radishes; cucurbits such as peas, beans, and other *Dolichos;* a great many aromatic and medicinal plants, and only three decorative plants: lilies, roses, and irises. The lily and the rose are often cited in medieval texts because of their religious symbolism: purity for the lily, associated with the Marian cult; beauty for the rose, whose thorns also evoke Christ's Passion. But flowers and their scents would have a truly important role only in the Renaissance.

Monastery gardens illustrate this predominance of sustenance gardens during the High Middle Ages. Like Saint Fiacre, the patron saint of gardening, an Irish monk who settled in Brie, monks were both clearers — the forest was never very far away — and gardeners. The Saint Gall monastery, founded in the Carolingian period near Lake Constance, with its beds of medicinal plants (the *herbularius*) and vegetables (the *hortus*) and its orchard (the *viridarium*) is the archetype of medieval gardens.

The monastic garden was surrounded by walls separating the cultivated land from untamed nature, order from chaos. It incarnated the good, the *gart,* the enclosed. The cloister was constructed around four paths intersecting at right angles and demarcating four plots of land. At the center of the cross thus formed there was a fountain or a tree. The number 4 symbolizes the four rivers of paradise, but also the four cardinal virtues (prudence, temperance, courage, and justice) and the Four Evangelists. The Christian symbolism of the cross is, of course, essential, as is the fountain, which evokes a holy water font.

Beginning in the twelfth century the garden as a theme was found in literature and art, revealing an evolution in its form and purpose. Always enclosed by walls or hedges, composed of geometrical beds sometimes raised and edged with trellises made of rush or thin strips of wood, covered with climbing roses on screens, sometimes containing a bench made of vegetation where one could sit, the medieval garden was organized around a fountain, creating an intimate, almost secret space. The *hortus conclusus* or "enclosed garden" would be associated by the Church with the virginity of Mary.

Such gardens are found in chivalric romances. The *hortus amoenus* was expected to unite the four elements and enchant the five senses. A single door, like an initiatory access, opened onto it, a theme picked up by Rousseau in *La Nouvelle Héloïse* and by Gide in *La Porte étroite.* But although the first part of the *Roman de la Rose* by Guillaume de Lorris contains a traditional, square garden, the second part, written by Jean de Meung, describes a circular garden, the ideal image of the cosmos and perfection. In that Eden one could abandon oneself freely to love, but also to poetry, philosophy, dance, or music. The "secret garden" would retain its erotic connotation for a long time: one need only imagine the copses of the grounds of Versailles and the labyrinth of the gardens of love . . .

More technical books, such as *Ruralia commode* by the Italian Pietro de Crescenzi, translated in 1373, contributed to the growing interest in gardens. The powerful were indeed interested in them. King Charles V had vast lands planted in what is now the Marais quarter—the street names there are their legacy: rue des Rosiers, rue de la Cerisaie or Beautreillis. Robert II, Count of Artois, having returned from the Crusades, created gardens famous for their automata (perhaps inspired by his stay in Sicily) in Hesdin, located in Picardy. Writers were not to be outdone: Dante, Petrarch and his property of Fontaine-de-Vaucluse on the banks of the Sorgue, near Avignon, and especially Boccaccio, whose *Decameron* is set in the countryside and in gardens where a group of ten young people fleeing the plague seek refuge.

This brings us to the Renaissance.

Gardens of Islam

Around 750 CE, the Abbasids, then the Almoravids, conquered a huge territory that, well beyond the Middle Ages, extended from Spain to India, from the gardens of the Alhambra to those of the Taj Mahal, from Al-Andalus to the Mughal Empire. The gardens of Islam continue in a straight line from the Persian paradises, but reflect a taste for geometry, abstraction, and above all the symbolism characteristic of Muslim art, inspired by a religious and philosophical conception.

Their design symbolizes an anticipation of a paradise where the four rivers of water, wine, milk, and honey, representing fertility and eternal life, flow freely. According to the Koran they separate the world into four parts. In the center, one finds the fountain, "the umbilicus of the world." A clever irrigation system enables the noncultivated parts to be covered with mosaics, out of which vegetation seems to spring forth. The shape of the rectangle separated by four canals opening into a central basin lends itself to countless variations. Grenada, Marrakech, Samarkand, Samarra, Baghdad, Isfahan, Lahore, and many other sites reflect this design, one that has endured over the changing centuries and civilizations.

GARDENS OF THE RENAISSANCE

Italy is the birthplace of the great gardens of the Renaissance, gardens built around villas and princely estates, primarily in the region around Florence, with its very sought after Tuscan land. Such lavish grounds were developed in the fifteenth century, following the desires of patrons such as Cosmo the Elder in Careggi or Pope Pius II Piccolomini in Pienza. They symbolized the power of those who commissioned them, for example in Castello, where the layout of the fountains reproduced the insignia of the Medicis.

Italian gardens were also the fruit of the thinking of the time, which encompassed an interest in antiquity as well as the most advanced research in the realm of science. Humanism rediscovered the ancients not to reproduce them identically but to reread them and connect them to the contemporary era. The influence of the Roman gardens of antiquity is clear, but it was enhanced by the informed work of architects such as Leon Battista Alberti (*De re aedificatoria* [On the Art of Building]), Niccolò Tribolo, and Giorgio Vasari (who would work at Castello, the residence of Cosmo di Medici), as well as by the newly acquired knowledge in mathematics and optics. Cicero's wordplay on the double meaning of *cultus* had never been so true: by cultivating one's garden, it was also one's mind and soul that were enriched.

The main departure from the medieval garden was that now gardens opened up onto the landscape. The garden of the Renaissance took into account the totality of the space in which it was situated. The varying relief of the land marked by terraces, woods, statues, fantastically shaped grottoes, waterfalls, and labyrinths brought together stone, water and the reflections of the sky, and the vegetation. All the senses were invoked, as in the fabulous water organ of the Villa d'Este in Tivoli, the Villa Lante at Bagnaia that so enchanted Montaigne, the gardens of Boboli or those of the Villa Pratolino. Fountains and waterfalls were among the essential elements of this scenography, inciting the passionate interest of a Leonardo da Vinci in water gardens. Increasingly, gardens were designed to engage the eye of the beholder, adopting a harmonious art of perspective.

Following Italy, all of humanist Europe became interested in gardens; they incarnated both a philosophy of existence and an art of living. In 1499 Francesco Colonna's *Hypnerotomachia Poliphili* (The Strife of Love in a Dream) described a garden with esoteric and metaphysical connotations. The Villa d'Este proposed several itineraries, one moral (one path led to vice, another to virtue), another esoteric, only for the initiated, under the allegorical aegis of Hercules. Four labyrinths symbolized the need to examine all realms of thought.

Erasmus, that eternal vagabond, in 1521 stayed for several months in Anderlecht. It was perhaps there that he wrote "The Religious Banquet" in which he proposes a variation on the garden of Epicurus—an ideal place where friends could live and philosophize together. And so the garden assumed a symbolic value, both Epicurean and Christian. Devoted to Jesus Christ, scattered with mottoes inscribed on signs, the garden was designed around a source of pure water. It was a place "designed as a pleasure garden, but for honest pleasure; for the entertainment of the sight, the delight of the nostrils, and the refreshing of the mind." Scented plants, grouped by species, grew in the beds there. The fences were painted green like a garden, arbors enabled one to read or to have meals in the shade, and, as in Roman gardens, trompe l'oeil frescoes rivaled nature. Behind the house, there was a vegetable garden and one for medicinal plants, which flowed into a field enclosed by a hedge teeming with entwined thorns, and an orchard. An aviary and beehives completed this "transcendental garden" (Michel Onfray), whose purpose was edification and pleasure. This paper garden was beautifully reconstructed a dozen or so years ago in Anderlecht and was opened to the public. I remember the spring day when some high school students came to have lunch on the grass, a couple was strolling arm in arm, a woman was reading near the river, another watched her baby. Everything was peaceful and alive. The beneficent spirit of Erasmus was watching over his garden.

Though it might appear more similar to the medieval concept, Erasmus's garden belongs to the Renaissance through the thinking that underlies it: beauty, philosophy, and spirituality are symbolically incarnated in this place. Nature and art are joined, giving birth to what the Italian theorists such as Bonfadio or Taegio called the *terza natura*—"third nature."

Filarete imagined an extraordinary garden labyrinth located

near an ideal city; the garden would have in its center a palace of plants decorated with hanging gardens evoking both Babylon and some of our modern buildings with plant-covered façades. Other imaginary gardens were conceived, such as that of Bernard Palissy, minutely described by that brilliant autodidact who was not just a ceramist but also a geometer, chemist, naturalist, and passionate gardener. That supporter of the Reformation who had asserted, "I have found in this world no more beautiful delight than that of having a beautiful garden," died in the Bastille after being tortured. His *Récepte veritable par laquelle tous les hommes de la France pourront apprendre à multiplier et augmenter leurs trésors* (1563)—quite a title!—weaves together all the themes of the Renaissance garden: geometry, the importance of water, the essential role of architecture, which transforms trees into columns and rocks into habitations.

If the Italians often favored the curved line, perhaps reflecting the undulating relief of Tuscany, the French at that time preferred straight lines, symmetry, "squaring." This tendency appeared at the beginning of the sixteenth century, with the gardens that Cardinal Amboise had constructed in Gaillon, in the *département* of Eure. Rectilinear pathways, right angles, geometrical shapes characteristic of the French classical style seemed already to be taking over, as at Anet, the residence of Diane de Poitiers, which King Henri II commissioned from Philibert de l'Orme. Architecture played a major role in the conception of those gardens, whether at Chenonceau, Ancy-le-Franc, Gaillon, Anet, or in the terraced gardens of Saint-Germain-en-Laye, created for Henri IV by the architect of the grounds, the gardener Claude Mollet, and the hydraulic engineer Tommaso Francini, the most extraordinary fountain maker of his time. In that latter garden, at the time considered to be the jewel of French gardening art, six large terraces extended from the chateau to the Seine, laying out a sumptuous landscape for the delight of royalty. Grottoes, fountains, and basins containing animated marvels, and flower beds portraying royal insignias, completed the whole.

Claude Mollet also redesigned the Tuileries Garden, which Henri IV wanted to connect to those of the Louvre. Mollet's *Théâtre des plans et jardinages* develops his theories and his method. In it he advocates borders of boxwood and mixtures of low flowers "like violets of all sorts, large and small daisies, wild carnations, double chamomiles, anemones, primrose, pansies." This blending "will represent the design of a Turkish rug."

Le Théâtre d'agriculture et mésnage des champs, by the agronomist Olivier de Serres, focuses above all on food resources and on mulberry trees for silk; its pages would inspire the agricultural policies of the duc de Sully. Serres experimented with those plants on his Pradel estate in the Vivarais region. But his remarks on the pleasure garden reveal the flowers that were held in highest esteem: the carnation, which was confused with the gillyflower, the tulip, and the peony. "Myrtle, lavender, rosemary, southernwood (a sort of privet) and boxwood are the best plants for borders"; they framed the aromatic plants: marjoram, thyme, wild thyme, hyssop, sage, chamomile, mint, violet, daisy, and rue, in spite of its somewhat strong odor. The colors of the plants and the ground were to be carefully chosen to highlight the combinations.

The perspective was essential. "It is desirable that the gardens be viewed from above, either from nearby buildings, or from raised terraces built around the flower beds."

The garden of the French Renaissance was indeed dominated by those geometrical compositions, those walkways that symmetrically configured the intricate flower beds more than they highlighted the dwelling place; the structures of greenery, of stone, and of water, all elements that paved the way for the "landscape gardeners" of the coming decades, in particular the greatest of them all, André Le Nôtre.

THE FRENCH GARDEN

Are French gardens rigid? Are Fontainebleau, Chantilly, Vaux-le-Vicomte, or Versailles monotonous, boring? You have probably not visited them for a long time . . . Leave the summer to the tourists and visit them in the autumn when the gold of the leaves is reflected in the waters of the Grand Canal, or in the winter when the snow reveals the contours of the flower beds, or in the spring when birds taking flight cause the copses to vibrate.

The embroidered flower beds; the mirrors of water where the changing sky of Île-de-France is reflected; vistas that seem to go on forever; fountains shooting their iridescent jets of water up to the sun; walkways in the shape of stars; hidden groves; dark masses of forests; the disturbing blend of symmetry and fantasy; carpets of vegetation unfolding as one walks along—all of this offers an unparalleled spectacle of a fusion of art and nature, a festival of the mind and the senses. These gardens are part of a unique moment in French culture, one that produced Descartes, Pascal, Molière, La Fontaine, and Racine, as well as Poussin, le Lorrain, Le Vau, Mansart, Le Brun, and Le Nôtre.

French-style gardens are the result of a number of factors, and the genius of a creator who was able to synthesize everything. Advances in the sciences that were occurring throughout the century, in particular the progress in optics and astronomy, altered a representation of space and of the place of man in the world, thus of his cosmic imaginary. Added to this were an increasing interest in science and mathematics, and the influence of Cartesianism. It was a unique era, one in which, around 1630, witch trials such as that of Urbain Grandier in Loudun existed alongside Descartes's *Discours de la méthode* and Baroque enchantment, the three unities of classical tragedy . . .

With Richelieu the centralization of royal power was achieved, with an accompanying weakening of the old nobility. The great estates were transformed, and gardens participated in this new movement. The most beautiful of them would be included in the monarchic project.

The foundational texts of this art of the garden were indeed offspring of the Renaissance, while they also emphasized the recent advances in the sciences. The engineer Salomon de Caus in 1612 wrote *La Perspective avec la raison des ombres et des miroirs,* highlighting the major role of water and optical illusions in gardens. Jacques Boyceau in his *Traité de jardinage selon les raisons de la nature et de l'art* encourages symmetry in the plant world, but also a prolonged vista and a mastery of proportions. Descartes's *Dioptrique,* the experiments of Torricelli, and those of Pascal in hydraulics would be put to use in the great fountains. As for André Mollet, his *Jardin de plaisir* traces the great lines of the French-style garden. Translated into Swedish (Mollet, like Descartes, was in the service of the queen of Sweden) and into English, it would contribute to the dissemination of this art throughout Europe.

But the most famous and the most talented of all landscape gardeners left no theoretical work, and almost no writings at all. The legacy of André Le Nôtre resides entirely in the gardens he created or in those to which he significantly contributed: Anet, Blois, Chambord, Chantilly, Fontainebleau, Maintenon, Marly, the Luxembourg, the Palais-Royal, the Tuileries, Saint-Cloud, Saint-Germain-en-Laye, Saint-Mandé, Sceaux, Vincennes, and of course, Vaux-le-Vicomte and Versailles. We must also mention the gardens in Berlin, Copenhagen, Greenwich, Windsor, Het Loo, Turin . . . and many others. In all, we know of more than seventy gardens in which Le Nôtre's collaboration is proven through documents, and dozens of others in which it is likely.

That grandson and son of gardeners to the king grew up in the Tuileries, for which his father was responsible. His path was set at his birth within a dynasty of men of the profession. His gardening classes were held alongside the best. Dyslexic, as is mentioned in his few written texts, Le Nôtre had a sure hand and a well-trained mind. He spent several years in the atelier of the painter Simon Vouet to learn drawing and the art of perspective. From that time he would retain a great sensitivity for painting, and his collections of works of art date from his first professional successes. The works of Nicolas Poussin and Claude Gellée, *dit* le Lorrain, are the jewels of that collection. Their influence is clear, in particular as regards composition and light. Le Nôtre also frequented scholarly circles. His career was brilliant and successful, thanks to his talent but also—no less essential—to his patrons. Gaston d'Orléans (the brother of Louis XIII), the Prince de Condé, many owners of large estates, and, above all, the superintendent of finances, Nicolas Fouquet, would soon commission important work from him.

With the help of the painter Charles Le Brun and the architect Louis Le Vau, Le Nôtre designed the gardens of Vaux-le-Vicomte, on which unparalleled technicians, such as the hydraulic engineer Claude Robillard, and Antoine Trumel, the chief gardener, collaborated. Le Nôtre perfected his method, which consisted of working brilliantly with the reliefs of the land using anamorphosis and a lengthening of perspective, as well as all the hydraulic resources of the site. It was a global conception that took into account both the difficulties of the terrain and existing buildings. The entire landscape would be remodeled, giving birth to the magic of thirty-three hectares of gardens. It would take twenty years to develop the estate, and a dozen years for it to be worthy of the celebratory *fête* of 17 August 1661, which came all too soon before the arrest of its owner, Nicolas Fouquet.

As someone who knew nature well, La Fontaine in the *avertissement* to his poem *"Le Songe de Vaux-Éloge des jardins"* recalls that it takes time for a garden to develop. Invoking the *Roman de la Rose* and the *Hypnerotomachia Poliphili,* he chose the latter literary genre to render believable his unexpected evocation: "Since the gardens of Vaux had just been planted, I couldn't describe them in that condition, unless I were to give a disagreeable idea of them, and which, after twenty years, would have most probably been unrecognizable." He sang the praises of "the orchards, the grounds, the gardens," the "crystal liquid" of the fountains. Before him, Madeleine de Scudéry, the author of *Clélie,* was already lauding Vaux: "the masterpiece of Art and Nature joined together."

They would have been very surprised at any objections to the regularity of the layout. Everyone who visited Vaux at the time was, on the contrary, surprised by the changing scenery that was revealed as one walked around, changes achieved through an astute mastery of the space. The symmetry does not consist in repeating identical motifs, but in balancing the two parts in order to simultaneously create an effect of variety and harmony. Patricia Bouchenont-Déchin sums it up ably: "Far from the static forms of the past, like the characters painted or drawn by Abraham Bosse, which the spectator views while looking over the landscape from a terrace or a balcony, the gardens of Le Nôtre are discovered by walking around in them; only then does the magic begin to work, and the lines, simple in appearance, in turn begin to move, revealing their depth and complexity."

In 1657, Le Nôtre became the general controller of the Bâtiments et Manufactures de France. Landscape designer and gardener to the king, he was also the architect of a space that he remodeled to better create it. He teaches us that a garden is always the result of an architecture of the landscape and work with the earth itself. "The great inventor of gardening," as the mathematician Christian Huygens called him, reigned over the most prestigious garden sites. Thanks to him, the Italian model was eclipsed. It was high time for King Louis XIV to put him to work in service to his glory. At Vaux, the monarch foresaw all the artistic and political profit he could derive from such talent.

Louis XIV was twenty-two years old. It would take twenty-five years for the chateau and the park of Versailles to take on their approximately definitive shape. The Grand Canal would only be dug in 1668, seven years after work had begun.

Gardens take a long time to develop. Tending a garden is not suited to the impatient. But we now have proof that Le Nôtre's overall plan for Versailles preceded the purchase of the land. He had to confront the difficulties of the site due to a lack of flowing water, the nature of the terrain, and technical and financial concerns. There was a visionary element to the "bonhomme" Le Nôtre. And a wonderful perseverance, as well, and the necessary flexibility when dealing with monarchs. It took hundreds of workers to transport the soil, to plant the thousands of trees along the pathways and the millions of shrubs for the beds and the copses, to dig the canal and the basins, to survive the malaria that raged in that swampy zone; it took many horses to pull the wagons, engineers to figure out the thirty kilometers of canalizations that are still in good condition today, fountain makers to bring to life the basins and the water jets, sculptors and metal founders to create the statues designed by Le Brun, and of course gardeners, the best, to cultivate the flowers, the delicate shrubs of the Orangerie, the fruit trees, the vegetables of the kitchen garden, to trim the delicate network within the flower beds, whose color varied depending on whether the base was sand, gravel, soil, or crushed brick, to maintain the walkways, the boxwood, and the lawns.

We must not forget the most essential element of all: the plantings. Pinkish jasmine and orange trees planted in the ground in the winter perfumed the walkways of the Trianon.

Madame de Maintenon expressed her wonderment in her letters: "Every night the flowers in the garden were replaced. One went to sleep surrounded by tuberoses and woke up to the scent of jasmine or gillyflowers. Every day something changed; it was as if fairies were at work arranging the grounds; where one had seen a pond the day before, the next day there was a copse; where there had been a forest, one found a hill, a reservoir, or a porcelain kiosk where one could take a light meal."

Le Nôtre oversaw everything. The king had confidence in him. They walked over the grounds together, and Louis XIV even wrote a manual of twenty-five points on "how to show the gardens of Versailles." "Childhood should be seen everywhere," he noted on an estimate submitted by Mansart, who also played an important role in the development of the gardens. The Dragon basin designed by Claude Perrault, or the labyrinth with thirty-nine fountains illustrating Aesop's fables and decorated with a quatrain by Benserade to instruct the Dauphin, are evidence that the king's wish was granted.

On this vast estate, which in the end would cover fifteen thousand hectares, there was also a Ménagerie, an Orangerie, and of course the wonderful Potager du Roi of Jean-Baptiste de La Quintinie, which alone merits a visit. Gardener, agronomist, botanist, this innovator would cultivate the early fruits and vegetables of which the king was very fond.

Everything worked together to place nature in the service of absolutism; the solar myth used by Louis XIV was the overriding principle. The first basin, then the crossing of the branches of the Grand Canal, and finally the last basin increase in size so that they appear to be of similar proportions. But their similarity is an optical illusion. The lengthy perspective that leads the eye to the horizon of the Grand Canal was created so that the sun would set there in all its glory on 6 September, the king's birthday. Using a clever calculation of proportions, the long walkways bordered by trees give a visual impression of regularity and alignment, while the long stretches of water below the Galerie des Glaces reflect the light and illuminate the façade.

Following the Apollonian and solar phase with its radiant walkways, beginning in 1674 statuary restored the quaternary theme, as ancient as the art of gardens: the four elements, the four seasons, the four parts of the world, the four temperaments (melancholic, choleric, phlegmatic, and sanguine), the four types of poems (heroic, pastoral, lyrical, and satirical), the four hours of the day, and, reconnecting with Eden and the theme of fertility, the four great rivers that watered France (the Garonne, the Seine, the Loire, and the Rhône). It was a statuary art inspired by antiquity, revealing a desire for organization and the stylization of classicism.

But one can understand and love Versailles only if one is sensitive to the astute play of shadow and light, the rustling of leaves, the rushing of water, to that full opera that combines all the elements, makes them play together, and exalts all the senses.

Le Nôtre had aimed for "beauty" and the "natural," faithful in that to the classical aesthetic. "In him, the triumph of intelligence had not destroyed the finesse of sensitivity," Henri de Régnier would note. As for beauty, who can deny its presence? His work is the reflection of the ideal of his time.

As a political project, the creation of a landscape, a place for the representation and the celebration of pleasure—hunting, parties, theater, music, walking, eating—Versailles spans the seasons and the centuries. As La Fontaine foresaw:

> As long as there are eyes, as long as we cherish Flore,
> The Nymphs of the gardens will incessantly praise
> This art that has lodged them so richly.
>
> (*Les Amours de Psyché et de Cupidon*)

Versailles was a model for all of Europe, an architectural ideal to attain, a political challenge for other rulers. And yet, those "gardens of intelligence" (Lucien Corpechot) would become the symbol of a conception that men at the turn of the century would reject, just as they would the classical aesthetic. It wasn't until the twentieth century that landscape architects and urbanists such as Le Corbusier, Henri Prost, or Sigfried Giedion would see it as a model for modern urban space. The grounds would inspire the National Mall in Washington, the Plan of Chicago, and the hanging flower beds of Rockefeller Center in New York, as well as many structures including the monument to the victims of September 11 by Peter Walker, who claimed to be fascinated by "Le Nôtre's work on the void." An unexpected legacy . . .

Le Nôtre as Seen by Saint-Simon

"Le Nôtre had a probity, an exactitude, and an uprightness which made him esteemed and loved by everybody. He never forgot his position, and was always perfectly disinterested. He worked for private people as for the King, and with the same application—seeking only to aid nature, and to attain the beautiful by the shortest road . . .

A month before Le Nôtre's death, the King, who liked to see him and to make him talk, led him into the gardens, and on account of his great age, placed him in a wheeled chair, by the side of his own. Upon this Le Nôtre said, 'Ah, my poor father, if you were living and could see a simple gardener like me, your son, wheeled along in a chair by the side of the greatest king in the world, nothing would be wanting to my joy!'" (Saint-Simon, *Mémoires*, 1700)

THE ENGLISH GARDEN

It is not yet the end of February, but the plum tree outside my window is already flowering. It took only a warmish night and morning for the buds to liberate their white petals. The branches stand out against the sky with the grace of an engraving. The garden is assuming a springlike look. Crocus, primroses, and daisies are flowering. Hyacinth and daffodils are swelling and pushing their necks out of the ground. New leaves on the stems of the hydrangeas signal the fall of wilted heads that I will soon remove. And, a marvel! Periwinkles . . . For me, their purple blue is the color of hope. I know, of course, that there will be some backward movement, that it could still snow or freeze up until May, but the days are getting longer and today I want to believe in the end of winter. The periwinkles always remind me of those in Les Charmettes, so dear to Jean-Jacques Rousseau. Like him, I can exclaim: "Ah! There is a periwinkle!" Be patient, Jean-Jacques, we will join you soon . . .

To do that we first need to travel to England. The history of gardens might be told only from the perspective of the active relationship between art and nature. A bit more art, and we tip to the side of the gardens of the Renaissance and the seventeenth century. A bit more nature, and we come to the parks of Romanticism. On the other side of the Channel the transformation seen in Italian and French gardens initially came up against fierce resistance. That resistance, under Dutch influence but following the model of medieval English gardens, culminated at the end of the seventeenth century in topiary art that gave birth, if I may say so, to the most extravagant shapes seen in the poor trees that lent themselves to it. In 1713 it took the humor of Alexander Pope in number 173 of the *Guardian* to ridicule that infatuation which was literally disfiguring nature by seeking to reproduce living beings. Citing the fantasist catalogue of a merchant, he listed:

Adam and Eve in Yew; Adam a little shattered by the fall of the Tree of Knowledge in the great storm; Eve and the Serpent very flourishing.

Noah's ark in Holly, the ribs a little damaged for want of water.

The Tower of Babel, not yet finished.

St. George in Box; his arm scarce long enough, but will be in a condition to

Stick the Dragon by next April.

A green Dragon of the same, with a tail of Ground Ivy for the present.

N.B. These two not to be sold separately.

However, England had already provided the art of the garden with the formal garden lawn, that sunken expanse of grass inherited from the bowling green, the lawn intended for the game of bowls. And England would offer Europe a major revolution, that of the irregular garden, also called an English garden, or landscape garden.

In order to understand the origin and the significance of the English garden we should look at the evolution that occurred in land ownership and the role of the gentry, the minor nobility, in the acquisition of the estates that were increasingly being made available to commoners. "New men take root in old land," wrote Daniel Defoe. Owners eagerly undertook to improve, embellish those properties which endowed them with additional respectability. Joseph Addison thus develops the image of the happy owner enjoying the benefits of a prosperity that he harmoniously maintains: "But why may not a whole estate be thrown into a kind of garden by frequent plantations, that may turn as much to the profit, as the pleasure of the owner?" (*The Spectator,* no. 414, 25 June 1712). Wood and underbrush for fireplaces, game for the hunt, fish for fishing, pasture for sheep and livestock, fruit trees: those huge estates did not just have an aesthetic function; they were also profitable.

And so some large properties would be modified by what today we would call landscape gardeners who would gradually invent a new style. They were the artisans of that liberation of the English landscape, contemporary with the new institutions that the country had just established. "Liberty and Property" was the slogan of the times.

In Stowe, near Buckingham, Charles Bridgeman then William Kent, a former designer who came to gardens thanks to his patron, Lord Burlington, invented the landscape park, bringing together lawns and the countryside. Kent designed ornamental lakes of irregular shapes and went so far as to plant dead trees to provide a more natural look to his compositions of copses.

In Storehead, the banker Henry Hoare made a triangular lake the heart of his garden. A footpath followed the gradients of the terrain while varying the lines of sight over the landscape.

The most famous of these landscape gardeners is probably Lancelot Brown, aka Capability Brown because he had the habit of saying to his (many) clients, "Your estates have great capabilities!" "The greatest gardener in England" (hundreds of gardens are attributed to him, which is probably an exaggeration) in turn redesigned the Stowe estate as well as Hampton Court for the king. His theory was based on three words: "belt," "clump," and "dot"; or a circular belt, copses, and isolated trees. And four elements: water, trees, the sky, and the ground. Undulating lawns continued right up to the door of the house. The circuit around the gardens was circular, but irregular, open to the inspiration and the whims of the visitor. The songs of birds, the shimmering of a pond, the hills, the scattered flowers, the rocks, all fed one's imagination and reveries. Discoveries were made at the rhythm of one's pace, one's observations. Brown's talent enabled sublimating the landscape, re-creating it by highlighting it.

Indeed, it was the landscape itself that was transformed into a garden. The "genius of the place" was to guide the gardener.

> Consult the genius of the place in all;
> That tells the waters or to rise, or fall;
> Or helps th' ambitious hill the heav'ns to scale,
> Or scoops in circling theatres the vale;
>
> (Pope)

Instead of perspective, the enlargement of the scale was now preferred; curves instead of straight lines; and ha-has instead of low walls. Surprise! The landscape now opened onto all of nature. An aesthetic "without lines and without level" (Pope) gradually took over. The garden was freed from geometry, which was associated by some with despotism. The "twisting" line prevailed even before William Hogarth in 1753 turned it into one of the canons of aesthetics in *The Analysis of Beauty*.

The garden became the privileged place of sensibilities. It was composed like a painting, by playing with the colors of the leaves, the shadows and light, the curves of the landscape. All the senses were to be invoked. As Christian Cajus Lorenz Hirschfeld wrote: "At a favored resting place, where we indulge our thoughts and fancies, where we would rather feel than observe, fragrant flowers should open their cups of sweet, spicy, refreshing scent, heightening our perception of the rapture of creation, through the satisfaction of a new sensation . . ." (English trans., 228).

The connections between painting and gardens became stronger. The Grand Tour, the ne plus ultra of a complete education and the initiatory visit to Italy, introduced and sensitized young English aristocrats to art. They visited Venice, Genoa, Rome, Florence, but also Naples, Paestum, Herculaneum, and Pompeii. They met with artists. They created gardens inspired by the works of Claude Gellée and Salvator Rosa. With Nicolas Poussin, the landscape assumed an essential place on the canvas. It was no longer a mere setting. One began to look differently at the nature to which painters, whether in the background or the foreground, drew one's attention. As seen later in Watteau, painters depicted for the most part gardens of a highly aestheticized nature. At the same time, a taste for neo-classical ruins and temples was spreading, and painters picked up on that. Some artists, such as Hubert Robert, would be both painters and garden conceptualists. With the title of "Designer of the King's Gardens," he was also one of the men in charge of the Louvre museum.

But the influence of the landscape garden can also be perceived in the novel, that new literary genre, whose developments, digressions, chronological structure that did not prevent returns to the past, multiplicity of vistas, evoked the freedom of the walker in the English garden. Writers such as Pope, Addison, Horace Walpole, and Rousseau were interested in gardens. We should also mention John Locke's reflections on the role of sensations in thought processes, those of Newton and the scientists for whom observation was crucial, and of Linnaeus on botany.

The great creation of a garden always assumes a synthesis of knowledge, tastes, and the sensitivity of an age. But it is also, of course, the result of observation and of technical work on the land. Between 1700 and 1760 a new form of art was born: the landscape garden. English gardening became "landscape gardening."

This conception of gardens was nonetheless the object of lively debates. For some, the aesthetics of a Capability Brown were too simplistic, worthy of the old gardener that he was. William Chambers, who had traveled in China, advocated a more conceptual scenario, in the image of Chinese gardens (whose spiritual dimension he didn't grasp), stressing the beauty and the emotional strength of their "vistas." Pagodas and hanging bridges became popular, and "follies" [*fabriques*], a term borrowed from pictorial vocabulary—false ruins, Greek temples, Gothic chapels—multiplied. As Monique Mosser notes, "It was no longer a matter of reproducing nature through a painting, but now the painting was projected, in true scale, *onto* nature." The "picturesque landscape gardener" thrilled theoreticians and practitioners: the garden became a fashionable topic, a profession of faith, an art of living. In England as on the continent, writers, artists, large landowners, and landscape gardeners were smitten. In the 1770s treatises and essays flourished. Within a few years of each other there appeared *Observations on Modern Gardening* by Thomas Whately, *Essai sur les jardins* by Claude-Henri Watelet, *De la composition des paysages* by René-Louis de Girardin, and the *Theory of Garden Art* by Christian Cajus Lorenz Hirschfeld, to cite only a few.

In France, Louis Carrogis Carmontelle was designing the Parc Monceau for the duc de Chartres; Hubert Robert was inventing Méréville; François Racine de Monville, the astonishing Anglo-Chinese garden, the Désert de Retz; and the marquis of Girardin, Ermenonville, where he hosted Jean-Jacques Rousseau. François-Joseph Bélanger created the "extravagant" garden in Neuilly, the Folie Saint James, that Claude Baudard de Saint-James commissioned from him, to rival that of his Bagatelle neighbor, the Count d'Artois. Bridges, kiosks, and pagodas put the spotlight on a steam pump–powered cascade that gushed out under the portico of a temple, itself built into a huge, twelve-meter-high grotto constructed with boulders brought from Fontainebleau. An underground labyrinth enabled visitors to hear the sound of the water and to enter the temple. At the time the grounds extended as far as the Seine.

At the end of the 1950s the Lycée de la Folie-Saint-James, which I later attended, was built there. We would walk through the grounds to have lunch in the outbuildings of the chateau. But the grounds served mainly as an athletic field. Every gym class began with a run around the park. Wearing the regulation blousy shorts, thighs reddened by the cold, I hated that jogging. The grotto that occupied the center of the park enabled me to escape the watchful eye of the teacher, who was standing still while our group passed on the other side. I would slow down or stop for a moment before continuing at a slow jog as soon as I was once again in sight, pretending to be out of breath. We practiced shot-putting not far from the temple of Love: quite a symbol! Did we appreciate where we were? We couldn't walk around or sit freely on the grass. The park was part of the school grounds, like a recess courtyard or classrooms. A garden is also what one makes of it. But in the spring, while looking through a window, I would dream, and in June, the scent of the flowers of the linden trees meant the coming of summer vacation . . .

...AND GARDENS
IN NOVELS

JEAN-JACQUES ROUSSEAU, OR THE INVENTION OF NATURE

Everything after him that has been written on nature is but a
more or less modified reflection of his influence.

—George Sand

I don't know why, but the story of Jean-Jacques Rousseau's
final weeks still moves me. A painful body, an ailing mind,
poor, solitary—even if some of his problems were due to the
bouts of delirium that had been seizing him for a long time—
the greatest writer of the century thus ended a tormented existence. Sapped by guilt and a sense of persecution, entrenched
in his pride, with only Bernardin de Saint-Pierre as a companion, he took walks, collected plants, and copied music to earn
his keep. He was very well known. But the time of struggles
had passed. After a life of wandering the hunted man could
finally rest. The very last lines he wrote, penned in the garret
that he shared with his wife, Thérèse, took him back to the beginning: "Today, a flower-filled Easter day, it has been exactly
fifty years since I first met Madame de Warens."

That sums it up. During his entire life he was that young,
fifteen-year-old boy, sheltered and helped by "Maman," his
protectress, his mother, his lover, who was thirteen years older
than he. He adds in what would be the tenth and final walk in

the *Rêveries du promeneur solitaire:* "A day does not go by that I do not recall with joy and tenderness that single and short time in my life when I was fully myself, without conflict or constraint, and when I could truly say I had lived."

He would never write again.

Soon, he wouldn't even be able to copy music anymore. He needed a refuge. The marquis de Girardin offered him a place to stay on his estate of Ermenonville. Jean-Jacques spent his final days there, at peace, gathering plants in the morning, walking with twelve-year-old Amable, his "little governor," rowing, or letting the boat drift along in the water. Reconciled with the world, with himself, he was finally "delivered from the anxiety of hope." He died on 2 July 1778, at the age of sixty-six.

His friend Bernardin de Saint-Pierre, who had looked for him in vain at his previous address, on the fifth floor of an apartment on rue Plâtrière, was saddened by his death, and looking at nature made him feel worse: "I felt I could see him on the unbeaten paths, at the foot of the trees, on the grass. The Pré Saint-Gervais, the Bois de Boulogne, Mont Valérien, the banks of the Seine, were echo chambers of his thoughts, I could almost hear his voice. When I went a bit farther, the plants themselves that covered the ground, and that he had introduced to me, seemed to say with each step that I took: you will never see him again" (*La Vie et les ouvrages de Jean-Jacques Rousseau*).

Jean-Jacques Rousseau was buried in the glow of the lamps on the Île des Peupliers, in the middle of the park of Ermenonville. The marquis de Girardin had a tomb placed there where the philosopher would remain until his ashes were transferred to the Panthéon in 1794.

Those two periods—the foundational stay at Les Charmettes and the final weeks at Ermenonville—to me, best reveal Rousseau's profound relationship with nature. From the little garden of Madame de Warens to the vast estate of the marquis de Girardin, through the Elysium of *Julie, ou la nouvelle Heloïse,* Jean-Jacques would transform the sensibilities of his contemporaries, and that of future generations.

Yes, we must begin at Les Charmettes. It doesn't really matter if that "brief happiness" was even more ephemeral than he describes it in book 6 of the *Confessions;* if, after he had settled in, Jean-Jacques was often alone while Maman stayed in Chambéry; if his stays with her were interrupted by departures, traveling, adventures. The time he spent there left its mythical mark on his memory and, in a certain way, on ours. Les Charmettes was a place of initiation: initiation into love, initiation into knowledge, initiation into music, initiation into nature. Happiness for Rousseau always corresponded to the moments when he was at one with himself: "I did what I wanted to do, I was what I wanted to be." Les Charmettes allowed him early on to experience the accomplishment of self. That country life would come to represent a sort of ideal that is found throughout his work. The garden is one of the facets of that ideal, an ideal that would encompass all of nature.

Jean-Jacques Rousseau and Madame de Warens spent spring and summer in the small house nestled on the side of the little valley: "In front was a terraced garden, a vineyard above it, an orchard below, opposite a small woods filled with chestnut trees, a fountain close by, higher up in the mountains, fields for grazing livestock" (*Confessions,* book 5). The lease was signed in July 1738, ten years after they met.

The house is still there, with its long garden and orchard. Thousands of visitors have passed through the refuge of Les Charmettes, which inaugurated the first literary pilgrimage, ever since Arthur Young went to gather his thoughts there in 1789. In 1792, the deputy Hérault de Seychelles went there with a delegation to place a plaque that is still on the front of the house: "Little house where Jean-Jacques lived / You remind me of his genius / His solitude, his pride / And his unhappiness and madness." Visitor books kept since 1811 include Lamartine, Stendhal, Sand, Rodin, Renan ("I have finally seen it, thank you, God, thank you"), Michelet, Anna de Noailles, Francis James, Paul Valéry, and many others closer to us in time: François Mitterrand and Robert Badinter. All, without exception, experienced the apprehension and emotion of George Sand, who went there with her partner, Alexandre Manceau, on 31 May 1861: "I didn't know if I would find what I had gone to look for there, and if the sight of things would fail to reflect the idea that I had had of it; but that fear faded as the carriage climbed slowly up that charming shaded road so well described by Jean-Jacques and so similar to what it had been in his time" (*Revue des Deux Mondes,* 1863). She even experienced a strange feeling of reminiscence when going into the dining room, as if she were rediscovering "a forgotten, yet still known place," she notes in her *Agenda (Diary).* Like her, we might say: "Les Charmettes are really mine now . . . I know on which garden path I will find the plants that I seek, I know those of the surrounding area, I know the stones on the path, I have a photo of the house in my head, I know the design of the upper part of the door frame in the salon and the notes that the spinet still plays."

As for myself, I know the periwinkle that grows at the foot of the house: it is sleeping between the pages of my old copy of the *Confessions*.

Book 6 of the *Confessions* contains an epigraph by the Latin poet Horace. Jean-Jacques Rousseau remembered: "I rose with the sun and I was happy; I took walks and I was happy, I saw Maman and I was happy, I left her and I was happy, I walked through the woods, the hills, I wandered in the valleys, I read, I was idle, I worked in the garden, I picked fruit, I helped with the housework, and happiness followed me everywhere; it couldn't be attributed to only one thing, it was entirely in me, it didn't leave me for a single moment." Those lines, in their clear serenity, paint a picture of happiness to which many would still subscribe. We are far here from the aristocratic ideal of salon society. To work in the garden, pick fruit, help with housework: all manual tasks, on the same level as walking or reading. His status as favorite did not exempt him from lending a hand, in the same capacity as Claude Anet, the valet (and lover) of Madame de Warens. In Rousseau's memory those activities illustrated the country life whose example he extolled. The garden of Les Charmettes, mentioned several times here, was small. All the same, in spite of his good intentions, his weak constitution did not allow him to work very hard. He had heart palpitations, ringing in his ears, insomnia:

"I was very sorry not to be able to tend the garden by myself; but after I had dug six holes with the spade I was out of breath, drenched in sweat, I had to stop. When I bent over the beating of my heart increased and the blood flowed to my head so strongly that I had to quickly stand up." And so the worker was forced to tend to the pigeon house and the beehives, or to do some light gardening when he had time. He derived just as much satisfaction from that. When the weather was warm he and Madame de Warens had coffee "in a cool and plant-filled room" which he had decorated with hop plants. "We spent a brief hour there visiting our vegetables and flowers." Rousseau, usually so precise when writing about plants, was vague. We will never know what was planted in the garden; the vegetable garden was of less interest to him than was nature as a whole. In the end, what enchanted him in his memory of Les Charmettes was the way of life there and, of course, Madame de Warens. In that valley his dream of a simple and happy life living in nature took root forever: it was his lost paradise.

He did, in fact, have an earlier experience with gardens. Jean-Jacques was around ten years old when he was sent with his cousin to the country, a few kilometers from Geneva, to the home of the pastor Lambercier. It was there, he informs us, that he first acquired a taste for the country life. "The countryside was so new to me that I could not tire of enjoying it. I acquired such a strong taste for it that it was never to dissipate."

He also discovered the friendship and complicity that united two active boys. Cultivating their little gardens, "scratching the earth lightly and crying out with joy in discovering the germinating seed" that they had planted, such innocent pleasures.

But one of Rousseau's favorite memories was the clandestine planting of a cutting from a willow tree, watered with the water that the two rascals diverted from a walnut tree that Pastor Lambercier had just planted. The pastor realized what had happened. A scandal! After two years, however, the countryside lost its charm for the boys, and they were sent back to Geneva. A year later Jean-Jacques began an apprenticeship with a notary. He was twelve years old. His childhood was over.

It's hard to imagine today the success that *Julie, ou la nouvelle Heloïse* enjoyed. Seventy-two printings of the novel before 1800 brought to life the thwarted love of Saint-Preux and his student, Julie. In it Rousseau gives free rein to his sensibility, to his dreams of love, to his love of nature, to his passion for philosophical debate. Far from being ethereal, the love that unites, and sometimes opposes, Julie and Saint-Preux is quivering with desire and sensuality. An epistolary novel that is sentimental and moral, granted, but carried by the force of an inspiration, a need for an ideal, that also includes long passages on the social subjects that were important at the time: the life of salons, the decline of mores, duels, family, the place of women, suicide, money, and the art of gardens. Thousands of readers identified with the characters, projected themselves onto the novel. Didn't Rousseau see himself in the hero, "giving him [. . .] the virtues and the defects" he observed in himself?

Rousseau had just moved into the Ermitage, a house that Madame d'Épinay was lending him on the grounds of La Chevrette, in Montmorency. A refuge like the one he had been dreaming about since Les Charmettes, surrounded by trees, far from the elaborate grounds and fountains of the chateau. Madame d'Épinay graciously had the house furnished for him, and he settled there with Thérèse and her mother on 9 April 1756. The song of the nightingale greeted him, the vegetable garden in front of the house provided vegetables, and, to repay his debt, he oversaw a large garden decorated with espalier trees, managing and ensuring its maintenance. Since the gardener was regularly pillaging from the fruit of his labor to sell the produce for his own profit, Rousseau's vigilance caught him in the act. Rousseau even got a dog, Duc, who would be a steady companion. But his days weren't spent entirely on the lookout for miscreants. Madame d'Épinay liked having him by her side at the chateau when she was alone—and he came running when she summoned him. He copied music, faithful to his decision not to live off his writing. He resumed writing his *Institutions politiques,* a text that he would abandon and radically rework into *Du contrat social.* His sentimental solitude, in spite of the presence of Thérèse, whom he never really loved, as he admits in the *Confessions,* led him to allow his imagination free rein. And so *Julie* was born. When he met Sophie d'Houdetot, Madame d'Épinay's sister-in-law, who had come to visit the reclusive philosopher on the advice of her lover, Saint-Lambert, things immediately became crystal clear: "The return of spring had doubled my tender delirium, and in my erotic transports I had written for the final parts of *Julie* several letters which emitted the ravishment in which I wrote them. Among others I can cite those of the Elysium and the walk along the lake." Thus, his work and life fed off each other.

Jean-Jacques Rousseau set the action of his novel on the

banks of Lac Léman, in Vevey, where Madame de Warens was born, a sort of final act of loyalty to Maman. But it was in Clarens, in the countryside, that Julie, then married and a mother, chose to settle with her husband, Monsieur de Wolmar. Saint-Preux, who meets her again after years of separation, thus encounters the family and the universe of the one whom he still loves. After talking about the economic system promoted by the physiocrats, one that enabled owners to turn a profit from the output of an estate while preserving the relationships between masters and servants, aristocrats and peasants, Saint-Preux tells his friend Lord Edward about his discovery of Elysium, Julie's secret garden.

Oh, what a secret! Meant only for Julie and those close to her, the door is always locked, it is invisible from the grounds, its entrance masked by trees. And so it is into a closed universe, entirely conceived by Julie, that Saint-Preux enters, and we behind him. This old orchard whose ground is a bit dry has been transformed into a luxuriant garden, "cool, green, cleared, flowered, watered." Flower beds, arbors, copses, trees, flowers and wild berry bushes. An enchanted garden that seems to have grown all by itself; but it is the result, in fact, of human ingenuity. Light alternates with the darkness of the undergrowth, wild flowers with those cultivated in the garden, branches seem to take root in the ground, flexible stalks wind like ivy around the trunks of trees, climbing plants, bitter nightshade, Virginia creeper, hop plants, bindweed, jasmine, honeysuckle and clematis, form fragrant garlands. A bit farther, there are clumps of wild roses, lilacs, hazelnut trees, syringas, broom plants that appear to grow at random. Grafting has enabled climbing plants to take root on the trunks of trees, reinforcing the impression of thickets and thick greenery. The Elysium in places resembles a woods, a sacred place of antiquity.

There is no symmetry, no straight paths or flower beds; sinuous paths go down to the bottom of the orchard, "serpentine" waters form a pool shaded by the willows where birds seek refuge: everything is done to charm the soul and the senses which the prose of Jean-Jacques Rousseau harmonizes without a wrong note. "You see nothing lined up," stresses Monsieur de Wolmar, "nothing leveled; a straight line never enters this place; nature plants nothing in a straight line; the windings in their feigned irregularity are arranged artfully to prolong the walk, to hide the banks of the island, and to enlarge the apparent extent without making unnecessary and overly frequent detours."

One of course thinks of the English garden such as the first great landscape gardeners, Bridgeman, Kent, or Brown, must have imagined it. Perhaps Rousseau had read Alexander Pope's "*Epistle IV*," *to Lord Burlington,* published in 1731: "Consult the genius of the place in all; [. . . it] paints as you plant, and, as you work, designs." Julie's Elysium is indeed nature reworked, reinvented, arranged with the goal of enhancing a place that was first without charm. But everything is done with a great economy of means, robust varieties are planted, hardy plants that need minimal attention to thrive, common species and not rare or exotic trees. Rousseau kept the essence of the English country garden but eliminated any subtleties or eccentricities. The Elysium is not the sumptuous park of an aristocrat, designed by an elite landscape gardener, but an intimate garden, reserved for Julie and her friends and family.

Rousseau was careful also to keep his distance from the different types of gardens that existed alongside each other in that mid-eighteenth century. He criticizes the Stowe gardens of Lord Cobham for their ruins, their temples, and the overly thought out assemblages of vegetation. But Julie's garden did borrow its name: Elysian Fields. Chinese gardens were considered too munificent, recherché and artificial. Moreover, the contemporary passion for tulips and horticulture is mocked: "those little curiosities, those little florists who swoon upon seeing a buttercup, bowing down before tulips." We may recall that the "tulipmania" that took hold of Europe in the seventeenth century ended in the trading of bulbs on the stock market. Well before Joséphine de Beauharnais and Pierre-Joseph Redouté popularized tulips at Malmaison, Rousseau was contrasting them to the rose, which was still a rustic flower: "The rose perfumes the air, enchants the eyes, and demands almost no care or cultivation. That is why florists look down on it: nature made it so beautiful that they are unable to add conventional beauty to it; and, not being able to torture themselves in cultivating it, they find nothing in it for which to flatter themselves." As for the French garden in which "the T square and the ruler" reigned, it was the antithesis of nature par excellence. "I am persuaded," says Rousseau ironically in a note, "that the time is coming when we will no longer want anything in our gardens that is found in the countryside: we will no longer tolerate in them either plants or shrubbery; we will want only porcelain flowers, grotesque garden gnomes, trellises, sand of all colors, and beautiful vases filled with nothing." There is nothing sadder, more pretentious, more artificial.

Not that Rousseau was against using art in the composition of a garden. But it was an art that should not be seen, "it is in hiding it that true taste consists, especially when it is a question of works of nature." The landscape gardener thus becomes a demiurge, but a modest demiurge who creates simplicity, the natural, a respect for the elements, "water, greenery, shade, and coolness" his main allies.

There has been a lot of debate as to whether Rousseau was at the origin of the fashion for landscape gardens. Of course, he was inspired by the first achievements of the English gardens, but kept his distance from the more ambitious of them. He had not yet gone to England, but had certainly read some pages of the abundant literature from across the Channel already devoted to gardens. He had seen engravings, paintings, like those of the Stowe gardens by Jacques Rigaud (*La Rotonde et le théâtre de la Reine à Stowe,* 1740). But he preceded by some dozen years the great treatises of his time, such as those by Whately or Horace Walpole (*On Modern Gardening,* completed in 1780, two years after Rousseau's death). The extraordinary success of *La Nouvelle Heloïse* contributed to disseminating throughout Europe a conception of the garden born in England, the way a seed is transported by a bird. Its strength comes from the fact that Rousseau had not written an abstract or technical treatise, but had incarnated his art of the garden through fiction and attractive characters in whom the reader recognizes himself. The magic of his prose did the rest.

I think that deep down he dreamed of his Elysium less as a theoretician than as a philosopher, less as a painter than as a musician. The babbling of the brooks, the rustling of the leaves, the songs of the birds, give life to the pages, and we seem to be walking on the mossy ground alongside the strollers. Julie's garden is a utopia, an imaginary garden in which Jean-Jacques placed his sensitivity and his philosophy. It incarnates an ideal of life. The Elysium is an Eden, an island of original nature—but created by the hand of a man, or rather, a woman. Julie dreams of one day handing it down to her children and teaches them to garden. Nature and Virtue: we are at the heart of Rousseauian thought.

Tell me about the garden you're dreaming of, and I will tell you who you are. When he returns to it alone the next morning, Saint-Preux finds in the Elysium something much more precious: serenity. Perhaps that is what Jean-Jacques Rousseau aspired to above all else.

The soul at peace; Rousseau found it in botany. In Montmorency he wrote *La Nouvelle Heloïse, Du contrat social,* and *Émile:* three works that had a considerable influence over his contemporaries and future generations, as well. Forced to leave the small house of Mont-Louis (the current Jean-Jacques Rousseau Museum), where he had taken refuge after his quarrel with Madame d'Épinay, the burning at the stake of *Émile, ou de l'education* and the warrant for his arrest again forced him to flee. He chose Switzerland, first Yverdon-les-Bains, then Môtiers in the canton of Bern, and he developed a taste for plant collecting there. He was persecuted again following the publication of *Lettres écrites sur la montagne.* His house was stoned, he was threatened. He sought refuge on Île Saint-Pierre. Once again, he thought he had found paradise, and botany became a passion for him. He even envisioned writing a *Flore* that would identify all the plants on the island. For the nomad Rousseau had become, such activity was the best remedy; it combined his love of nature, walking (he was a great walker), and analysis. It kept him from falling prey to the deliria of his wild imagination. In fact, Madame de Warens had attempted once to interest him in that science, but since he felt it was associated more with the herbalist shop, his young man's perspective turned it into "an apothecary's study" of little interest. Maman, who was very astute, nevertheless envisioned creating a botanic garden at Chambéry.

During the Enlightenment, botany was becoming a true science thanks to progress in optics and the work in nomenclature by Carl Linnaeus, whom Rousseau greatly admired. It went hand in hand with the evolution of both sensibilities and reason. Botanical gardens were developed, illustrating the rise of science and nature.

However, the philosopher wasn't interested in studying botany as a scholarly subject, much less for its medical side, but, as he wrote in *Les Rêveries du promeneur solitaire,* for the pleasure of walking, of reverie, and of reminiscence. The seventh walk is devoted to the theme: "Plants seem to have been planted profusely on the earth like the stars in the sky, to invite man through the attraction of pleasure and the curiosity of studying nature." The entire earth had become a garden. Even in Paris, Jean-Jacques would find enough to study by examining the most common plants that grew around him. An early urban ecologist, he notes: "With each blade of grass I encounter, I say to myself with satisfaction: here again is another plant."

Rousseau was a true botanist, he assembled dried flower collections, corresponded with specialists, built a significant library, which he would be forced to sell. He communicated his passion beyond his time, notably through his *Lettres élémentaires sur la botanique,* published in 1782 thanks to the efforts of the marquis de Girardin. These eight letters had been written at the request of Madeleine Boy de la Tour, the wife of the banker Étienne Delessert, for her daughter Madelon. Very lively, they are written as a pedagogical dialogue. They would travel around Europe and would provoke a true infatuation for the subject.

In *Émile,* the person who suggests botany to ladies because it is far from abstract speculation confides that it has become "a sort of passion that fills the void of all those who no longer have any." His final weeks at Ermenonville are devoted to it. Iconography shows him holding a bouquet of flowers, as in the oft-reproduced engraving by Georg Friedrich Meyer, or in that watercolor in which his hand is in that of the little Amable, the old man being led by the child . . .

The marquis de Girardin envisioned turning his huge estate into a philosophical park in homage to Jean-Jacques Rousseau and to the Elysium of Julie. It took eleven years, from 1766 to 1777, to drain the swamps and shape the landscape. This masterpiece of the picturesque garden on which the architect Jean-Marie Morel and the painter Hubert Robert had collaborated was conceived by René de Girardin as a spiritual and moral journey. Granted, it was more ornate and thought-out than its literary model, and scattered with some fifty structures, temples, and stelae of philosophical content . . . But, to

71

the north, the section called the Desert was perfectly wild and romantic, and in many ways faithful to Julie's garden. Things had come full circle. I hope that Jean-Jacques lives on there as a symbol and a culmination. Unless, quite simply, he was enthralled to find there one morning, hiding in the undergrowth, a periwinkle . . .

"I returned to Ermononville," wrote the Prince de Ligne, "I believe I cried. I blessed the historian. I sat on his bench" (*Coup d'oeil sur Beloeil,* 1781). Just a few years after Jean-Jacques Rousseau's death, pilgrims flocked there from all over Europe. Queen Marie-Antoinette, Joseph II of Austria, Jefferson, and later Bonaparte, came to reflect before the cenotaph designed by Hubert Robert on the Île des Peupliers. De Girardin had "a monument to former loves" built there in memory of *La Nouvelle Heloïse.* The cult of "the Man of Nature and Truth" had begun.

We Must Cultivate Our Gardens

The conclusion of *Candide* is inseparable from Voltaire's move to Ferney in 1759. "All that we know how best to do on this earth is to cultivate it," wrote the philosopher, who would devote himself to improving his new property on the Swiss border. A proponent of science and technology to improve yield, he wrote articles for the *Encyclopédie* entitled "Agriculture" and "Fertilization." He even had a little plot of land that he cultivated with his own hands: "Monsieur Voltaire's field" or "Voltaire planting a tree" popularized in the form of engravings and paintings the image of the philosopher-gardener. They didn't detract from his main objective, which was to develop his land and improve the lot of peasants. While Candide's optimism is quite relative, cultivating the twenty acres that he shared with his friends was "the only way to make life bearable." Thus the famous phrase should be taken literally as well as figuratively. In its way, this collective garden was the philosophical ancestor of the workers' gardens of Abbot Lemire at the end of the nineteenth century, which became collective gardens in 1952. The very popular gardens of inclusion and urban gardens—might they not be the distant heirs of the Lord of Ferney?

GEORGE SAND, OR THE NATURAL GARDEN

> We are of nature, in nature, by nature, and for nature. Talent, will, genius, are natural phenomena like the lake, the volcano, the mountain, the wind, the star, the cloud.
>
> —George Sand, letter to Gustave Flaubert, 8 July 1874

Nature is everywhere in George Sand. In her writing and in her life. In her novels, in her autobiographical texts, in her letters, in her flower collections, but also in the "dendrites," those landscapes created from pigments or ink spots retouched with paint, and of course, in her gardens. From the pot of mignonette on her windowsill in Paris, to her bohemian days on the grounds of her property in Nohant, or later, in Palaiseau with Alexandre Manceau; from the bouquets of flowers that she picked to decorate her house to the plants that she dissected and observed under a magnifying glass; flowers and gardens were hugely important to her. Her passion for nature was linked to her profound conviction that we are, as she wrote to Flaubert, "from and for nature." Nature in all its forms interested her, and not only on the domestic front. Traveling in Italy, Switzerland, or Majorca, walking in the public parks in Paris, her gaze would linger, her mind analyze, her pen describe. Her curiosity was endless. She didn't just sing the praises of gardens in her novels; botany, entomology, mineralogy—she was genuinely interested in it all. Gardens were thus a very small part of her immense desire to know and to do. Because she wasn't content simply to contemplate, to learn, or to dream. That incredibly active woman was also a "doer." Her body and her mind were not separated. That is what brings her so close to us. She had a "determination to address herself to life at firsthand," as Henry James wrote in *George Sand.* She liked to sew, embroider, cook, draw. And also to garden. Far from being exhausted after digging a little with a spade, like Rousseau, of whom she was a disciple, she found in gardening a relief to her anxiety, a cure for her sadness. If we are to believe *Histoire de ma vie,* she had a melancholic, even depressed side to her. Gardening enabled her to regain contact with vital natural forces. Nature was the fundamental principle of her presence in the world.

Although George Sand was enthralled with all the concrete aspects of gardening, she showed little interest in kitchen gardens, except for the vegetables that were eaten each day in Nohant. The garden there was the domain of the gardener, or the peasants. Moreover, both were idealized in her writings. Her tastes were aligned with her milieu, that of the Parisian aristocracy, for whom the property in the Berry was originally a country estate, bought by her grandmother in 1793. She spent her early years in Paris, but was raised in Nohant. Her life was a series of comings and goings between the Berry and Paris, which she didn't like. After the Revolution of 1848 she moved to the country for good. She kept a pied-à-terre in Paris, but went there only from time to time. She clearly saw herself as a country landowner.

"Every day, she would walk around her garden and visit her plants. She loved them, guided them, raised them up as she passed by. She knew the date they emerged, the places where their beauty would be enhanced, the way to take care of them," wrote her granddaughter Aurore Sand, in her *"Souvenirs de Nohant."* The *Agendas* are a record of her work in the garden. She ordered fruit trees, supervised plantings, and picked bouquets for the house, listing the flowers—this was also a way of remembering what grew each season. Thus, the winter of 1852 must have been particularly mild, since she notes for 18 December: "Bouquet picked in the garden: Bengal roses; white and flesh-colored tea roses; mignonette, double violet gillyflower, a scabious, fragrant *tucilage* [*sic*]; violets, hazelnut roses, verbena, valerian, snapdragons, primroses, wild periwinkle, a final hollyhock, laurel, thyme, flowers of Hautbois strawberries, ivy leaves of mixed red and yellow." Her passion for flowers is always evident in her great descriptive precision.

What was essential was to "learn to see." Her favorite flower was the cabbage rose of her childhood. Cultivated varieties didn't yet exist and wild roses covered the woods: "canina, thus named because it was believed to be a remedy for the bite of a rabid dog; cinnamon rose, musk, *rubiginosa* or rusty rose which is one of the prettiest; scotch rose, rose myrtle or cotton rose, alpine rose, etc., etc." The pleasure of listing, the pleasure of *naming.* "In our gardens," George Sand continues, "we had charming varieties that have practically disappeared today . . . : a red and white mixed bloom whose petals were quite sparse, but which showed its crown of stamen of a beautiful bright yellow and which smelled like a bergamot orange. It was quite hardy, enduring both dry summers and harsh winters; the pompom rose, both large and small, which has become excessively rare; the little May rose, the earliest and perhaps the most fragrant of all, which today one asks for in vain in the shops; the Damascus rose or Provins rose which we knew how to grow, and which now can only be found in the south of France; finally, the cabbage rose or, to be more exact, the 'rose of a hundred petals,' whose origin is unknown and which is generally attributed to cultivation. It is this centifolia rose that was then, for me as for everyone, the ideal rose . . ." (*"Ce que disent les fleurs,"* in *Contes d'une grand-mère*).

Today, the garden in Nohant includes a rose garden, a justified homage to George Sand's passion: "I adore roses," Sand wrote to the novelist Alphonse Karr, "they are the daughters of God and of man, lovely beauties of the field whom we have turned into incomparable princesses." Her favorites were a thorny white rose with small petals and the white tea rose with a greenish center, which can endure frost. Thanks to Joséphine de Beauharnais and her Malmaison estate, as well as to the talent of Joseph Redouté, who illustrated the prodigious varieties collected by the empress, roses became the darlings of gardeners and enthusiasts. The nineteenth century was crazy about them, as it was about all flowers, products of culture as much as nature. They were invited into elegant interiors, such as, for example, Madame Récamier's "nun's cell," where a large white rose bush immortalized by the painter François-Louis Dejuinne in his painting *Madame Récamier à l'Abbaye-au-Bois* held sway. Chateaubriand also described the window and the pots of flowers, looking out over the nuns' garden . . .

George Sand used flowers as ornaments, as decoration— for example, the bouquet in her hair in the famous portrait by Eugène-Louis Charpentier—or as a motif in the pieces she embroidered in the evenings for the armchairs in her sitting room.

She also encouraged Delacroix to paint them: "I saw Eugène Delacroix try for the first time to paint flowers. He had studied botany when he was young, and, since he had an admirable memory, he still remembered what he had learned, but it hadn't struck him as an artist, and its meaning was revealed to him only when he carefully reproduced the color and shape of the plant. I surprised him in the throes of delight when he realized the beautiful *architecture;* that was the wonderful word he used" (*Nouvelles Lettres d'un voyageur*).

It's no coincidence that George mentions botany. Here, too, she appears as a perfect child of a century that, in the footsteps of Jean-Jacques Rousseau, was enthralled with that branch of the natural sciences. The Jardin du Roi, today the Jardin des Plantes, was enhanced with new species, courses were given there, scholars vied for the privilege of dethroning Linnaeus's organizational system for naming plants. "The thinking of our times aims to have us love nature," George Sand notes in *La Rêverie à Paris.* For her, botany was not the insignificant occupation of a young girl, but represented a deep understanding, among other things, of the sexual reproduction of plants, and therefore, beyond that, an understanding of a part of the universe. It was also a different way to observe nature, no longer being content simply to contemplate or admire it, by seeking meaning in its organization. She never stopped studying: "Can you find out from some specialist—you must know quite a few—what is the most recent, and the most complete work in botany of all those that have appeared recently? And if it's really expensive? And where it is sold? I have Lamarck and Candolle, Boreau, Boiteau [sic], Mérat and Boisduval. None of them talk about exotic plants, and it is impossible to understand the connection of things in nature without filling that gap," she wrote to the publisher François Buloz in August 1860.

In *Le Pays des anémones,* a text devoted almost entirely to the subject of botany, she gives a true lesson in plant collecting: how to dig up a plant without making it suffer (because who can tell us that plants don't feel things? she wondered), how to "throw" it and not place it in paper so it will maintain a natural pose, how not to crush it, to observe it under a magnifying glass, and so forth. Of course, herbariums were "cemeteries," she agreed, but it was like "the passing of a human life through nature, the enchanted voyage of a loving soul in the beloved world of creation." Dried flowers also remind us of the moments of serenity we experienced while picking them, the cherished people who gave them to us, such as Deschartres, her father's old tutor, who guided her first steps as a botanist, or, above all, Jules Néraud, aka le Malgache, her childhood friend to whom she dedicated the fourth of the *Nouvelles Lettres d'un voyageur.* That great traveler, a former lawyer and justice of the peace, had devoted his life to botany. Paying homage to him in *Histoire de ma vie,* George Sand happily tells of their first encounter when at sixteen she saw dahlias for the first time in his garden. Getting off her horse, she picked one and set off at a gallop! Le Malgache gallantly sent her some dahlia bulbs and—do we need to point this out?—fell madly in love with the pretty flower thief . . . without ever being paid back.

Let us now return to the garden itself. Of course, to maintain the rather large property George Sand needed the services of a gardener. But she was not averse to working in the garden herself. In the *Agendas* kept by her final companion, Alexandre Manceau, we see her vigorously planting orchids and violets, ivy and holly. "How sad that you can't see the leaves and the flowers grow day by day! Every morning it's a delight to open one's window and see the progress that the night has wrought. It rains a lot and the river is full. But it is so mild and so cool that we don't mind. I am gardening furiously. I have a spade, a wheelbarrow, watering cans, a rake, etc., etc., all of this for my use and the right size for me," wrote this mite of a woman of "four feet, ten inches" to her oaf of a son, Maurice. She was gardening "furiously"? Yes, that nonchalant woman described by her contemporaries as a "sleepwalker" was capable of an energy that came from the depths of her being. She watched over her garden even in the winter. "Madame is doing very well, and to take a bit of exercise she moves the snow in front of her with a rake and with such energy that she is as warm as in the month of August," noted Manceau with amusement on 28 December 1853. She was almost fifty years old, a canonical age. But that's the point! It was her way of fighting against her years, and against "the revolution of age" that brought hot flashes and migraines. It was true therapy. "I work in the dirt four or five hours every day with the passion of a madwoman, and I have created my dream garden in my little woods," she wrote to her publisher Pierre-Jules Hetzel, from whom she hid nothing, or almost. ". . . all the stones that I turn, all the stumps I dig up, the watering cans, the barrows full of gravel and dirt, all the plays, novels, little nothings that I dream of while doing it, intellectual wanderings—it's wonderful." And she concludes: "It's because I work with my head as much as my body. It is an obsession and I turn positively to monomania." And this wasn't a flash in the pan, because her undertaking, a garden for her beloved granddaughter Jeanne, called Nini, would last months. No, there was absolutely no separation between the head and the body of this woman, even if, she admitted, "letters do not give [me] half the pleasure the spade does."

But the garden of Nohant, of course, was also a place for walking and for gatherings of family and friends. Friends from the Berry and from Paris, famous people and the curious, enjoyed the great freedom they found there strolling through the grounds while the mistress of the house worked or rested. Who hasn't dreamed, when visiting Nohant, of those evenings when, on the terrace, Franz Liszt and Marie d'Agoult chatted with George Sand while listening to Frédéric Chopin play the piano . . .

Gardens were also deeply rooted in George Sand's life, from the time when she was still called Aurore Dupin. Her mother, a rather flighty, coquettish woman, the daughter of a bird merchant on the banks of the Seine in Paris, is described in the *Histoire de ma vie* as having "a true intuition of the poetry of the fields, a love and a talent for gardening." The garden was inscribed in the maternal line and its popular roots. One of

Aurore's most wonderful childhood memories is connected to that whimsical mother, who placed her under the care of her detested mother-in-law. During a stay at Nohant, she created for her daughter a grotto of stones and seashells, a miniature version of the Anglo-Chinese garden in fashion at the time, which enchanted Aurore. When she was a bit older, Aurore in turn undertook to build, under the branches of three maple trees in the deepest part of the thicket of the same little woods, an altar of stones, shells, and moss taken from the stream, decorating it with flowers and leaves, and dedicating it to Corambé, that idealized imaginary being.

And she would in turn introduce her granddaughter Nini, born to the stormy couple Solange and the sculptor Clésinger, to the joys of gardening. Alexandre Manceau helped her to create a garden in the little woods. They emphatically called it "le Trianon." Just as Aurore once did, Nini gathered shells and moss to decorate the grotto: "she digs, she rakes, she hauls, she is developing a very strong little body." Grandmother and granddaughter "Trianonned" with a vengeance. The day when Manceau surprised them with a magnificent fountain, Aurore's transfigured childhood magically resurfaced. Tragically, Nini died when she was six years old, and that was the only time in her life when George could not bear the sight of her garden in Nohant.

Other childhood memories were connected to gardens, such as that of her aunt Lucie in Chaillot, which at the time was still in the country. She was four years old. That little rectangular garden, very long, surrounded with walls, planted with vegetables and flowers as of old, didn't prevent her child's imagination from flying. A born landscape gardener, she also composed "magical landscapes and gardens" by listening to the fairy tales that her mother would read to her, and entered into creation through that route. "There were green, black, purple roses, blue roses above all." That blue rose of which Balzac is said to have dreamed for a long time . . . "I saw illuminated thickets, fountains, mysterious depths, Chinese bridges, trees covered with gold and jewels."

Those childhood inventions were quite far from her adult aesthetic, however. Like Pope and Addison, she held to a respect for the "genius of the place." And so she criticized Madame de Béranger, a friend of her grandmother, for having once taken advantage of the woman's weakened state to have an English garden created at Nohant on land and with vegetation that were not suited for the project. Built in the eighteenth century for the governor of Vierzon on the site of a former fortified castle, Nohant at the time had a classical garden, with its plots of vegetables and flowers. On the side of the La Chartre road, the grounds are enclosed by a wall and bowers, and on the other, it is open and continues into the woods. The terrain is flat, without a view, the vegetation is heavy. Madame de Béranger, persuaded she had a genius for landscaping, convinced the ill grandmother to let her carry out the operation. Directing some twenty workers from her window, she had trees cut down, sought in vain to create a vista where there was only a great farmed meadow, and destroyed the little bit of shade that was there. "It took thirty years to reverse the damage Madame de Béranger did to our place," George Sand concluded bitterly, "and to close the breaches of her *vistas*." Standing in front of the painting by Eugène Delacroix *Le Jardin de George Sand à Nohant* (1842), we can say that she succeeded very well. A thicket with a grassy expanse in the distance, a stone table under the branches of a cedar tree (perhaps one of those that Sand planted when her children were born), and huge foxgloves give that romantic setting a country touch.

But for Sand, "the garden without walls and without cultivation" remained "the ideal garden." Sensitive to the harmony between the environment and the garden, to an opening onto the landscape, George Sand, like everyone in her century, liked grounds that were both organized and natural. She offered as an example the garden of Monsieur Turette on the tip of Antibes (today the magnificent Botanical Garden in Cap d'Antibes), a true Eden between the sea and the mountains, the most beautiful she had ever seen for its location and composition. Whether Sand is describing "the wild gardens" of Majorca she visited with Frédéric Chopin (*Un hiver à Majorque*), or those in Italy where she strolled with Alexandre Manceau (*La Daniella*), she liked a certain abandon to render poetic the overly rigid look of an elaborate composition. Above all, she was sensitive to the landscape, to the flower beds, to the variations of light and color, the scents, the songs of birds. Sensuality and reverie. Balance and simplicity.

Several times in the *Nouvelles Lettres d'un voyageur,* she develops the idea of the "natural garden," a prophetic conception that Gilles Clément, the author of *Éloge des vagabondes,* has echoed. The "natural garden" for Sand did not refer to a landscape composition that imitated nature, but to a preserved space where nature itself evokes a garden. In her opinion, the

so-called landscape gardens were only decorative gardens—
however extraordinary they might be, such as the new public
gardens in Paris. Their exotic flora was presented as "an artistic summary of creation" and a precious educational tool
for the public. But if "you want to see the garden of creation"
don't go to the end of the earth, she suggested. It was there,
everywhere in France, in ten thousand unknown places . . .
(*La Rêverie à Paris*).

"Instead of planned and cared-for gardens I prefer those
where the earth, itself rich in local plants, allows the complete abandon of some parts, and I would happily place plants
into two camps, those that man alters and transforms for his
use, and those that grow spontaneously. [. . .] They are much
more delicate, much more precious for science and for art,
those *weeds,* as they are called by farmers and gardeners. [. . .]
The passion for horticulture is making so much progress that
gradually all the primitive types will perhaps disappear like the
primitive type of wheat that has disappeared. Let's enter re-
spectfully, then, into the sanctuaries where the mountains and
the forest hide and protect the natural garden" (*Nouvelles Lettres
d'un voyageur*).

Was that simply a romantic view of nature? An early form
of ecology? No, not really. The term "sanctuary," the verbs "to
hide" and "to protect," refer to another function of the garden
for George Sand: as a refuge. A place that opens one to reverie,
to one's imagination; it is also a place of escape and comfort in
the solitude of a circumscribed space. Following a dispute with
her grandmother or later with her husband, the obtuse Casi-
mir Dudevant, she would go deep into the garden to collect

herself. Later, there was a similar scenario: "I remember one day when, revolted by nameless injustices that assailed me personally from several directions at the same time, I went to cry in the little woods in my garden at Nohant, to the place where once my mother made for me and with me her sweet little rock gardens" (*Histoire de ma vie*). That day, without knowing why, full of bitterness, she picked up a big stone and dropped it while sobbing: "Ah! My God, I might have another forty years to live!" After two hours of despair, calm gradually returned. She was ready once again to carry on: "Resignation is not in my nature." After the death of her granddaughter, she retreated alone to the chalet of their "Trianon" to think of her, and to cry.

The garden, like all of nature for Sand, also encouraged contemplation, meditation, even a spiritual experience. Sensitive to all that pulsed and lived, Sand experienced a pantheistic fusion with the universe. Written in simple prose, the *Agendas* reflect those moments of peace found in the garden, as on 12 April 1854. A wonderful coincidence: I am writing these lines on 12 April 2014, 160 years later. Nothing has changed: "The evening is magnificent, a full, or almost full moon. [. . .] The moon is above the island. The leaves of the linden tree are emerging, leaves are appearing on the hawthorns and on the lilac bushes, too. Those of the large path in the garden are flowering. The nightingales are singing at the top of their lungs. The new green is like a vapor spreading under the woods and the moon is making the periwinkle shine like blankets of water. A rare evening for the season. Finally, it's *spring*."

How could gardens not find a place in Sand's novels? Sometimes they appear in a descriptive pause, sometimes in a profusion of poetic prose; they are found in most of Sand's novels, either in their rural form as in the country tales or in *Mauprat,* or in a more refined form, as settings for an amorous encounter or a dialogue. Made wild, like the neglected grounds of the chateau de Blanchemont in *Le Meunier d'Angibault,* gardens participate in the dramatic atmosphere and in the action itself. The ditches, the scrub, the rabbit warren invaded by stumps and underbrush, form the landscape of the "mad woman" who wanders looking for her lost love. A realm of madness, of pursuit, of the loss of bearings, the setting plays a significant role in the economy of the novel. The old seigneurial estate, left to ruin during the Revolution, also symbolizes the decay of an aristocracy on the ruins of which the socialist utopia of the novel would be constructed.

Through a garden one sees not only the social adherence of its owner but also his character, his tastes, and even his political or social aspirations. In a certain way, it plays the role of the house in Balzac's novels. In *Mauprat,* which is structured entirely around floral motifs and gardens, the final metamorphosis of Patience, the hermit, is incarnated in her garden, which has returned to order and fertility: "Splendid vegetables spread out in straight lines like an army on marching orders." Rows of cabbage, carrots and lettuce, apple and pear trees, herbs at the foot of sunflowers and gillyflowers "betray in Patience a singular return to ideas of a social order and habits of luxury." In *Le Péché de monsieur Antoine,* the estate of Boisguibault, which became a "socialist garden," now serves the communal utopia. It represents the end of privileges, the sharing of property and wealth, collective work. It would become the "*garden of the commune,* that is to say also its gyneceum, its feast and banquet hall, its theater and its church." The novel ends with this profession of deist and pantheistic faith by Monsieur de Boisguibault: "I have put in the trees and in the flowers, in the streams and in the rocks, in the prairies, all the poetry of my thoughts. Do not take his illusion away from the old planter, if illusion it is! He still believes in that adage that God is in everything and that nature is his temple!" George Sand could have made that her credo.

And so it is not surprising that the garden becomes a metaphor for the work of the writer herself. "I write the way I garden," says George Sand, and again in a letter to the actor Bocage, somewhat casually: "I have beautiful flowers in my garden and I still scribble books easily" (1843). As for her memoirs, they are "a garden that is more difficult to dig in" than the Trianon intended for Nini (6 May 1853). In a letter to Victor Hugo, she says the same thing: "I cultivate for myself my 'little literary garden,' as Dumas would say, and the expression pleases me greatly, I who am enthralled with botany. My novels are pages of a herbarium." True or false modesty, it doesn't matter. I note above all the coherence of George Sand's universe. The garden and writing, botany and literature, were facets of the same creativity, and a celebration of the same love of life. Reasons enough for me to celebrate her!

We shouldn't be surprised, either, that her final words, murmured in a dying breath, were: "Leave . . . greenery." I hope that wherever she is, the gardener of Nohant can still wield the spade and the rake, and pick a few plants for the herbarium of the angels. . . .

A Passion for Flowers

Following Jean-Jacques Rousseau's *Lettres sur la botanique,* the nineteenth century exhibited a true passion for botany and horticulture. Publications abounded throughout Europe, such as the *Gardeners Dictionary,* or monographs and almanacs devoted to flowers. Botany was the first science to be open to women. The empress Joséphine played an important role in this. She corresponded with scholars from the Muséum d'histoire naturelle, had cultivars imported, encouraged expeditions such as that of Nicolas Baudin to Australia. More than two hundred rare plants are attributed to her, including the purple magnolia, the tree peony, the hibiscus, the phlox, the camellia, the dahlia, as seen in the work written by Étienne Pierre Ventenat and illustrated by Pierre-Joseph Redouté, *Le Jardin de la Malmaison.* She surrounded herself with the best specialists, such as the botanist Aimé Bonpland, who was made steward of the estate. At La Malmaison 250 known varieties of roses were cultivated, most of the time in pots that were taken outside when the weather was good.

Joséphine, who was born on Martinique, had a true passion for nature; it was the precursor of that of her century. Romantic parks were filled with new exotic varieties. *Le Langage des fleurs* (1819) by Charlotte de La Tour promoted the symbolism of love in flowers (Balzac would use it for

Le Lys dans la vallée). The journal *Le Bon Jardinier* devoted more than eight hundred pages to trees, horticulture, and the sexual system of plant reproduction. The *Revue Horticole, Journal des Jardiniers et des Amateurs* contributed to an expanding knowledge. The profession of landscape gardener renewed ties with its gardening roots (now there were "gardenists"). The combination of the sciences taking off and Romantic sensibilities gave birth to a new approach to nature, one that was inseparable from culture.

LOVE IN THE GARDEN
Balzac, Stendhal, Flaubert, Hugo, Zola

Sitting on a moss-covered bench until the hour
of sunset, busy telling each other great nothings,
or enveloped in calm . . .

—Honoré de Balzac, *Eugénie Grandet*

From the biblical Eden to the *Thousand and One Nights,* from
the *Roman de la Rose* to *Paul et Virginie,* gardens have been associated with couples and with love. Representations have ranged
from the idyll and purity, sensuality and libertinage, innocence
and the Fall. With Romanticism, continuing in a straight line
from Jean-Jacques Rousseau and a celebration of nature, the
garden became an irrefutable motif in the nineteenth-century
novel.

Honoré de Balzac's *Le Lys dans la vallée* illustrates this phe-
nomenon perfectly. It will serve as a touchstone for this visit
of a few literary gardens, true microcosms of the universes of
their authors. This is one of my favorite novels, I admit. I will
thus give it a place of honor at the heart of the flowering literary profusion of the nineteenth century.

In *Le Lys dans la vallée,* nature and the characters are inseparable. Balzac uses that identification to create both narrative

and poetic effects. Indeed, the title sums up the metaphor of the woman-flower, which is developed throughout the book. The landscape that surrounds the heroine is in her image, and the hero, Félix de Vandenesse, recognizes this even before *knowing* it: "If a woman, the flower of her sex, inhabits a place in the world, that place is here." The landscape is not only the setting of the story but a separate, unique "place" that announces, embodies, and symbolizes the beloved woman.

Félix de Vandenesse, a young, introverted man who is ill at ease in society, is seized by a violent erotic impulse when he meets Blanche de Mortsauf. In the grip of an irresistible desire, he kisses her and rolls his head between the uncovered shoulders of that unknown woman, seated next to him at a party. What an extraordinary start to a novel! That desire would be the secret motor, the flame that animates the platonic love she imposes on him and makes it pulsate. We discover at the very end that the same desire was devouring her. Madame de Mortsauf is married to a horrible man, with whom she has two children. She daily endures the injustices of that domestic tyrant whose only excuse is a nervous illness and who, in spite of everything, feels affection for her.

At the beginning, Balzac "thought of giving a wonderful role to the landscape." He tells Léon Gozlan: "Consumed with that idea, I plunged into natural pantheism like a pagan. I became a tree, the horizon, stream, star, fountain, light." In fact, nature washes through the novel, which takes place in Touraine, Balzac's native region. The childhood and youth of Félix have many points in common with those of the author.

In a famous description of the landscape at the beginning

of the novel, "a magnificent cup of emerald at the bottom of which the Indre flows, winding like a snake"; a nature made up entirely of curves, sensual, feminized, and described with lyricism, serves as a backdrop "for the woman who shone in this vast garden." Her white percale dress can be seen under a peach tree. Her first name is emblematic. Blanche is "THE LILY OF THIS VALLEY where she grew to the heavens, filling the valley with the fragrance of her virtue." The entire book is saturated with floral metaphors. The garden scenes are not just simple descriptive pauses or narrative parentheses. They are inscribed with the very economy of the story; they create its core and its structure.

We enter into the little chateau of Clochegourde with the narrator, Félix. On the valley side, to the south, the glass door opens onto a double portico that leads to the terraced gardens and, farther, to a meadow along the Indre. The last level is shaded by a double line of acacias and Japanese ailanthus. A sunken path bordered by hedges separates it from the meadow, which, seen from above, seems to be part of the gardens. These topographical details play an essential role throughout the story. The terraces overlooking the Indre open like a stage over the landscape; they are the theater of the love between Blanche and Félix.

On the courtyard side, "there is a wide graveled path onto a grassy lawn decorated with several flower beds." Nothing but the everyday, no description: this part of the garden scarcely interests the narrator who, on the other hand, lingers over the vineyard and the orchards that encircle the estate up to the banks of the Indre. The enclosures, the vineyards, and the walnut trees are an intermediary combination, both agricultural and familial. While enlarging the actual garden of the property, they represent the responsibilities of Madame de Mortsauf, whom the neglect of her husband secretly forces to oversee the estate, and situate the sites and the characters within their social and economic contexts.

The garden is a space that is both intimate and open to the valley, the opposite of the house, a place that is either social (the parlor, the dining room) or private (the bedroom), thus forbidden, except at the very end of the novel. The garden is also an indicator of time. The narrative unfolds following the seasons, each of which gives a tone to the vegetation and to feelings.

The first amorous conversation takes place in the evening, at the end of the month of August, when Félix, seated on a brick balustrade on the terrace, hears the sounds of a stormy exchange between husband and wife. Blanche then joins him, and during an intense scene they exchange confidences about their unhappy childhoods before concluding a pact that comes straight out of a scene of courtly love. This pact is a true baptism: he drinks her tears, she allows him to call her by the name which her godmother gave her: Henriette. While talking they walk around the terrace two times, then she opens the little door at the bottom of the terrace for him, the one that opens onto the sunken path and the meadow. In a movement that is symmetrical to the initial description, and a technique of high- and low-angle "shots," she watches him from the terrace where she has returned, while Félix, on the path, sees "her

94

white dress illuminated by the moon." What could be more romantic!

A second scene, which parallels the previous one, takes place a bit later, under the acacias, in the setting sun. The count has gone to bed and the children are playing around Félix and Blanche. In silent, or almost silent, communion, they savor the peace of the nightfall that casts orange light onto the bricks of the balustrade. An almost familial tableau, if not for Félix's increased desire. He caresses Blanche's hand, she pulls it back, then places it herself on the lips of the young man. "I dared tell her that at my age, if the senses were all soul, the soul also had a sex." She refuses herself. He promises to be good. Blanche de Mortsauf is a Madame de Rénal who won't give in, and Félix a Julien Sorel mad with desire.

The novel then expands over the entire valley that the young man travels in order to make bouquets for his "dear one." They will speak the language of flowers in his place. Two blue and white bouquets, then wild flowers throughout the months of September and October: "No declaration of love, of uncontrollable passion could convey more vehemently than these symphonies of flowers; my thwarted desire led me to employ the same effort that Beethoven expressed in his notes: a profound reflection, a prodigious movement toward heaven."

Balzac told of how difficult it was for him to obtain botanic details about the flora in Touraine. This descriptive parenthesis unfolds over several levels. The first is connected to the narrative through the symbolism of flowers. Like a painter, the novelist chose them for their colors: lilies, white roses, cornflowers, forget-me-nots. A blue and white bouquet, with Marian colors . . .

The second level is explicitly connected to "a more profound study less as a botanist than as a poet." The culminating point of the evocation is a piece of descriptive bravura, a euphoric hymn to passion and to the "red desire of love." We are indeed in the realm of literary representation—"a poem of luminous flowers" that isn't seeking a realistic effect but is rich in erotic connotations: "From the depths of this prolific torrent of love bursts forth the magnificent scarlet poppy, its pistil ready to open . . ." Balzac couldn't be clearer! The wealth of the lexicon of flowers, their precise nomenclature, create an impression of profusion, fecundity, equaled only by that of impulsive feelings. This secret language used only by the lovers overwhelms them. For the moment.

Félix picks those flowers in meadows and woods, moors and forests—beyond the enclosed and sacred space of the garden. Only the topography of the garden interests Balzac, because it enables him to frame the narrative and the position of the characters in relation to each other. The space is structured vertically (the terraces) and horizontally (the enclosures, the vineyards). But, unlike the bouquets picked in nature, we know nothing about the flowers that fill the beds and the pots. Only a few trees are named. Félix's erotic passion can only be expressed freely, wildly in a way, beyond the carefully tended space of the Mortaufs' garden. The entire landscape constitutes a romantic park. The bouquets that Blanche places in vases in the parlor and in her room are secret emissaries of love.

With autumn comes Felix's departure. A final stroll on the

terrace "under the naked trees" marks the end of the first period of love. Félix de Vandenesse leaves to pursue his career in Paris, with only a long letter of advice from Madame de Mortsauf as a viaticum.

When he returns the following May, he again finds their "dear valley" and their "dear terrace." Blanche comes back to life under his gaze, "like the effects of the month of May on the meadows, like those of the sun and the rain on wilted flowers." But that rebirth doesn't last long. Félix now lives his life and his loves in Paris, far from Blanche, as she herself advised him to do. The spirited Lady Dudley is his mistress. During his next visit, he discovers a distant Blanche on the terrace. But their dialogue gradually resumes. "She looked at me from under the warm rays of the setting sun that was sliding through the leaves, and stricken by I don't know what compassion for our broken love, she plunged back into our ever so pure past, allowing herself to return to mutually shared thoughts. We recalled the past, our eyes went from the valley to the enclosed fields, from the windows of Clochegourde to those of Frapesle, populating the reverie with our fragrant bouquets, the story of our desire." Their love was already in the past tense, the garden was only an echo chamber for what once was. "It was her final sensual pleasure," the narrator adds. Blanche has become aware of her wasted life. Their final stroll occurs under the flowering acacias, but in a final renunciation, Madame de Mortsauf avoids prolonging it into the night.

Félix would see Blanche only once more, the following autumn, when she calls him to her deathbed. The countryside is empty, the moor dried out, the garden neglected, the paths untended. After a burst of delirious life when she confesses her passion to Félix, Blanche dies. "The murmuring of the evening, the melodious rustling of the leaves, the final chirping of the birds, the chorus of buzzing insects, the babbling of the water, the plaintive cry of the tree frog: the entire countryside said good-bye to the most beautiful lily of the valley, to her simple life in the country." That lyrical good-bye is the final homage to the woman he loved. The entire novel is, in fact, based on what is not said between the two lovers, on forbidden words, on the signifiers of a deeply shared language that assigns nature, and sometimes silence, the task of expressing that which cannot be said: their desire.

The garden of Clochegourde, with its descending terraces, overlooking the meadow and the river, thus opens onto the landscape of the Indre valley and continues into it while still being distinct from it. Throughout the novel it plays the role of romantic literary garden, both an indispensable place for narrative progression and a social and historical signifier taking its place in Balzac's *Études de moeurs*. The balustrade, the sunken path, the shadow of the acacia trees, the enclosed spaces—they represent a confinement that encourages intimacy, but also that which is forbidden. It is a feminine landscape, reflecting the mistress of the place; it emerges from the domestic space (the husband, the children) *and* from the garden of love and voluptuousness, the *locus amoenus* of the lovers. But, while it enables amorous intimacy, it makes the fulfillment of desire impossible. It is the vast estate of Madame de Mortsauf, but also her prison. It is predictable that right before she dies, in a final burst of delirium, Blanche reveals her erotic passion to Félix, saying she wants to flee Clochegourde with him and go to Italy, the quintessential refuge of lovers. Blanche de Mortsauf had a bit of Emma Bovary in her . . .

Le Lys dans la vallée (1836) and *Le Rouge et le Noir* (1830) were almost contemporary. I like that Balzac was one of the rare writers not only to salute Stendhal's novel when it came out but to rank it next to his own work, *La Physiologie du marriage,* in a movement that he called the "school of disenchantment," in his opinion, emblematic of the year 1830. These works signaled "the genius of the times, the cadaverous odor of a dying society" ("Lettre XI sur Paris," 10 January 1831, *Le Voleur*).

"The sinister and dark philosophy" of *Le Rouge et le Noir* is apparent at the very beginning of the novel in the famous garden scenes, which are tempting to reread after the lyrical effusions of *Le Lys dans la vallée,* published, let us remember, six years later.

Monsieur de Rénal owns two gardens: that of Verrières, which on two occasions in the first chapter is described twice, rather flatly, as "magnificent." Like Clochegourde, it features terraces descending to a river, the Doubs, and separated by walls. "In Franche-Comté," Stendhal notes, "the more walls one builds, the more one sprinkles one's property with stones piled on top of each other, the more respect one earns from one's neighbors." Moreover, one of those parcels was bought at a high price from old Sorel, Julien's father. The "magnificent gardens" of Verrières are thus the reflection of the *magnificence* of Monsieur de Rénal, his money (he owns a company) and his power (he's mayor) as a notable in a small provincial city. The gardens have no other function than to show the extent of that money and power—a source of irony for the author.

Monsieur de Rénal's other property is in the countryside, in Vergy. The mayor, mimicking courtly habits, goes there with his family at the beginning of spring. The garden is "designed like that of the Tuileries, with strong borders of boxwood and paths lined with chestnut trees trimmed twice a year." There is nothing very poetic here, although the description provides a supplementary reference to the royalist ideas of Monsieur de Rénal, since the Tuileries surround the royal residence. Like the walls of the terraces, the boxwood borders and the trimmed chestnut trees also reflect the rigid character of Monsieur de Rénal, a firm supporter of order.

The grounds have a rustic feel, with a field of apple trees, an orchard that culminates in a thicket of walnut trees. As in *La Nouvelle Heloïse,* Madame de Rénal is already secretly in love with Julien, the young tutor of her children (Saint-Preux was Julie's tutor), and has a gravel path put in, transforming the orchard into a romantic garden of which Rousseau's heroine would have approved. The vista, Stendhal insists, rivaled that of the mountains of Switzerland and the lakes of Italy. A few meters away, there was a wild and even "sublime" landscape that overjoyed Julien, walking with Madame de Rénal and her friend, Madame Deville (reminiscent of Julie and her friend Claire).

Closer to the house, under a large linden tree, one of Julien Sorel's first conflicts would be played out in several stages. However, all the conditions seem perfect for a scene of romantic love: a summer night, a stormy sky, "the rustling of the wind in the thick branches of the linden tree." But far from being caught in the throes of love, Julien is obsessed by the challenge he has set himself: to take Madame de Rénal's hand. That which overjoys the woman represents only a "duty" for the man. Four successive scenes under the linden tree will enable Julien gradually to increase his advantage to a final victory: in Madame de Rénal's bedroom.

We can see how Stendhal undermines the stereotype of the romantic idyll in the garden. Entirely self-absorbed, Julien is unable to participate in the union into which Madame de Rénal plunges with happiness and fear. The shade of the linden tree, the charm of the summer night, are for him only the propitious setting for a new victory. Julien, who is very young, can still only find happiness in himself. "The school of disenchantment" is indeed also one of "truth, the bitter truth" (the novel's epigraph). It is only at the end, not in a garden but in a prison cell, that Julien Sorel will finally experience love for Madame de Rénal.

By employing the motif of the garden after Stendhal did— let us recall that *Le Lys dans la vallée* came later—Balzac used almost explicitly the scene of the linden tree in *Le Rouge et le Noir* while moving it under the flowering acacias. Everything was there, even the terraced garden. But in *Le Lys dans la vallée,* the novel and lyricism have taken over: the characters' love is shared, if not consummated. We shouldn't be surprised that Balzac had more female readers than Stendhal did . . .

Blanche de Mortsauf's renunciation turns her into a passive victim who dies of anorexia for not having given in to her desire. That romantic descendant of *La Princesse de Clèves* guided young Félix de Vandenesse, to whom La Comédie humaine would later offer a brilliant career under the July Monarchy. The "flower of her sex," she remained forever buried under the foliage of her garden at Clochegourde.

Madame de Rénal discovered passion under the linden trees of Vergy and ruined her reputation before she died—she, too, of love—three days after Julien Sorel was executed. One woman resisted, the other gave in, both failed. At least Madame de Rénal experienced a few moments of happiness while visiting Julien in his cell even after he had shot her. In both cases, the garden was a theater of conflict and an antechamber of loss.

The garden does indeed constitute what Michel Foucault calls a "heterotopia," a place beyond all other places and in which "all the other real sites that can be found within the culture are simultaneously represented, contested, and inverted" (English trans., 24). As such, it is the placement in space not only of the action but of the very meaning of the novel. Both inside and outside the house, it plays the role of mirror. The little garden of Père Grandet in *Eugénie Grandet,* with its "thick, humid walls full of seepage and tufts of scrawny bushes," represents a shrunken place, closed, stifling, untended. All the sordid greed of Grandet, his love of secrets, the absence of a horizon from that tight provincial life, are reflected in it. Nature cannot flourish in it—except through the eyes of a young girl in love.

The day following the arrival of her cousin, the handsome Charles, Eugénie can find new charm in that sad landscape: "The harmonies of her heart merged with the harmonies of nature." A ray of sun illuminates "the '*cheveux de Vénus*' [maidenhair] with thick, drooping leaves of changing colors, like the breast of a pigeon," adding a sensual note to the hair of the young girl who has just combed it. Throughout the novel scenes are focused on the mossy wooden bench on which Eugénie exchanges tender words with Charles. It is a bench of love, and will later be one of solitude when she sits on it to read the letter of farewell that Charles wrote to her while humming a Mozart melody.

The letter of farewell from the Parisian dandy is echoed by that of the provincial seducer, Rodolphe Boulanger, in *Madame Bovary,* who drips a drop of water instead of a tear on his letter. There is the same provincial garden, in spite of the more rural setting; a similar "bench made of rotted wooden planks," on which Emma Bovary spends feverish hours under the moon with Rodolphe; the same illusions: for one, the return of the beloved; for the other, a departure with her lover . . . And in the end, there is the same cruel disappointment. It is also in this garden, on the same bench, under that same arbor, that Charles Bovary—another Charles!—would spend his days after the death of Emma, and would one evening fall, "his face up against the wall, his eyes closed, mouth open," with a long lock of black hair in his hands. In the meantime, the jasmine and the Virginia creeper have bloomed, the white lily has grown. It is summer. Poor Charles!

For Balzac and for Flaubert, a few details were enough to establish the setting: rickety steps, three paths, plots of earth, a few raspberry bushes, a walnut tree, the dead November leaves at the Grandet residence; at the Bovary's, an arbor, a jasmine, a vineyard. Everything is merely mentioned, because what is important in these gardens is less nature itself than the scenes that are played out in them. The garden's charm is only an illusion. The enchantment doesn't last. The garden is only the setting for ephemeral sentiments or even for a lie. It is also revelatory, as seen in the way the novelist inscribes it in the dramatic and psychological progression of the story. The garden ends up incarnating, fixing the multiple meanings of the novel, assembling them into a single and tragic image of solitude: Blanche contemplating the valley from her terrace; Eugénie Grandet sitting forever on her bench in the back of the garden; Charles Bovary ending the novel as he opened it. Only the image of Madame de Rénal and Julien Sorel, hand in hand under the linden trees, anticipates that of their final union—in prison and death.

How tame they appear, those provincial gardens with their gravel paths and their flower beds, their linden trees, their walnut trees and their acacias! The giant, Victor Hugo, would shake the trunks of the trees and transplant a virgin forest within the walls of a Parisian garden, in a reinvented street as true for us as it was for his characters. Did it come from his memory of the parc des Feuillantines of his childhood? Of the street of the same name where his father was living when he died? In a chapter of *Les Misérables* entitled "Foliis ac frondibus" (Leaves and branches), the great voice of Victor Hugo celebrates "the sacred effort of things toward life."

The garden on the rue Plumet has been abandoned for fifty

years. In order to protect the hideout where he is staying with Cosette, Jean Valjean leaves it untended. Out of this garden, protected by a rusty padlocked fence, Hugo creates a "colossal underbrush," a marvelous jungle, and beyond that, a symbol of nature and fraternity. A stone bench, one or two mossy statues, a few broken-down trellises, but more paths, grass, and flower beds. The eighteenth-century park, the theater of libertine games, has disappeared. Two pages of poetry, powerfully animated by verbs of movement, oxymorons, antitheses, lists, comparisons, periods replaced by semicolons, an ascending rhythm, anaphoras, transform the garden sometimes into a beast in heat tossing its green mane, and sometimes into an astonishing festival of all the senses celebrating "universal germination," "the holy mystery of its fraternity, a symbol of human fraternity." Life in its entirety breathes in this garden, that of the infinitely large and that of the infinitely small, every species, from a blade of grass to man, from the gnat to the jellyfish. Everything comes together in the great egalitarian myth. The garden of the rue Plumet becomes the symbol of a universe in perpetual gestation in which all creatures collaborate, from the weakest to the most powerful. Indeed, this is the great lesson of *Les Misérables*. It is in that Eden that Marius and Cosette will secretly live their passionate and chaste love: "What happened between those two beings? Nothing. They adored each other."

Thirteen years later, in 1875, *La Faute de l'abbé Mouret* was published. Through the story of Serge Mouret, a young, twenty-five-year-old priest, Émile Zola wanted to study "the struggle of nature against Catholicism," the battle between the sun and the shadows. Le Paradou, a vast garden that had been returned to wild nature, would serve as the setting for Serge's rebirth through the love of Albine. Even if the context, the story, and the main thematics are different, it is difficult to imagine that Zola, who once admired Hugo's work but then became increasingly critical of it, was not thinking of the idyll on the rue Plumet at the time he conceived his Paradou. As in Hugo, nature is animated with a powerful movement of germination, of growth. Plants and men are moved by the same mechanism of life. But everything is amplified in Zola: the two pages in Hugo become several complex, descriptive, detailed chapters, which also borrow from the style of Michelet.

The enclosed garden is a recurrent motif in Zola; we find it in stories such as *Le Bain* (a garden that had been abandoned for a hundred years), in *La Fortune des Rougon, La Conquête de Plassans, Une Page d'amour,* and *Le Rêve.* These places of contemplation, of communion between people, provide a protective space apart from the world, shelter the emergence of an innocent love, common themes in the world of literature.

But these paradises are also enrooted in Émile Zola's personal mythology: the memory of the "paradou" of his childhood in Aix, a world of freedom and of fusion with nature that he describes in *L'Oeuvre:* "It was an escape far from the world, an instinctive absorption into the heart of good nature, the irrational adoration of children for trees, water, hills, for that limitless joy of being alone and free." What the young boys— Zola, Baille, and Cézanne—experienced in an open space on the banks of the river Arc, his characters would discover within the protective confines of an enclosed garden.

Zola wrote *La Faute de l'abbé Mouret* during the summer of 1874 in the house he shared with his mother and his wife, Alexandrine. He himself was not averse to working in the garden next to the house, wearing a sweater and an old pair of pants. His friend Paul Alexis wrote: "I remember two or three times when he would read on site from the novel he was writing, at dusk, in the stifling little garden surrounded by high walls behind the house."

Le Paradou came out of that little garden. But it is so huge that its edges can no longer be seen. Zola's biography reveals the important place it occupied in his imaginary. He would give its name to the chalet he had built on Île du Platais, across from the Médan property he purchased two years later with the proceeds from his very successful *L'Assommoir.* And the tree of life in the novel would be reproduced by the master glassworker Henri Babonneau on the huge window of the billiard room in the house. Nature in its original form in *La Faute de l'abbé Mouret* intersects with the genealogical tree at the foundation of the entire structure of the *Rougon-Macquart: Histoire naturelle et sociale d'une famille sous le Second Empire.*

It is under the branches of that tree of life that Serge and Albine experience love. The tree is the apogee of the garden; to discover it takes a long journey. As in Genesis, it presides over a loss of innocence. The long descriptions of the other parts of the garden—the rose woods, the flower beds, the meadows, the old orchard—are constructed from a nomenclature that suggests there were preliminary files containing lists of names of plants that were checked off as they were used in the text. Zola also used specialized catalogues and visited horticultural exhibitions. It is perhaps that research which, paradoxically, often makes his descriptions seem somewhat artificial.

However, Zola claimed above all to have been inspired by the Impressionists: "Those painters helped me to paint in a new way, 'literarily.' [. . .] But with *La Faute de l'abbé Mouret,* I plunged into the supreme peace unique to nature and thereby purified all the drama of the *Rougon-Macquart.* [. . .] It has been claimed that I created Paradou out of the paradisiacal park of Monet where his wonderful paintings were born. Whatever the case, both came together in the wild abundance of leaves and flowers."

The play of colors and shading, of the reflections of light, of shadows in the folds, of transparency, occupies an important place in the descriptive technique, and concurs with the rhythms, the sonorities, and the images, making certain passages true poetic paintings in prose. And yet, do the aesthetics dominate the narrative content? Le Paradou has meaning only in relation to the evolution of the two characters and to the structure of the narrative. Except, instead of simply signifying chaste love at one with euphoric nature, as in Hugo, the reference to the myth of the Garden of Eden prefigures original sin. There's no need for a tree of the knowledge of good and evil, as in Genesis, nor of the tempting serpent. Within the primitive harmony there insinuates "the intolerable anxiety" of desire. The tree of life, personified as a paternal giant, represents "the very virility of the earth." The lexical field of sensuality intersects that of nature. As a new Eve, Albine incites Serge to love, but it is the garden itself "that wanted the sin." The text celebrates the "victory of the beasts, the plants, the things, that wanted the entrance of these two children into the eternity of life."

But once the fullness of love has passed, there comes the fall and the expulsion from paradise. The garden, far from being only a setting, a narrative, or even a poetic element in *La Faute de l'abbé Moret,* carries all the symbolism of the text and the fundamental ambiguity of sexuality for its author.

Another novel, *La Curée,* explores this movement more deeply. Greenhouses made their appearance during the Industrial Revolution and at universal expositions. Those in the Jardin d'Hiver on the Champs-Élysées, inaugurated in 1846, or that of the Crystal Palace in London, conceived by Joseph Paxton around 1850, drew huge crowds. Greenhouses became an indispensable luxury accessory for rich individuals smitten with exoticism and rare plants. There were two in Zola's garden in Médan. In the Saccards' greenhouse (*La Curée*), exotic plants, carnivores, proliferate in an overheated and damp atmosphere, "an exuberance that only the iron framework could contain—as morality is meant to contain our impulses." The greenhouse accentuates the characteristics of the garden; its overheated atmosphere brings them to enhanced paroxysms. Renée, a modern Phaedra, seduces her stepson, Maxime. Nature in this stifling microcosm engenders a perverse and deadly enjoyment that, here too, can only lead to a fall. The greenhouse became a recurrent theme in novels at the end of the nineteenth century, as in Maupassant where it appears in a ribald (*La Serre*) or crazy (*Un Cas de divorce*) way.

Le Paradou of *La Faute de l'abbé Mouret,* as well as the greenhouse in *La Curée,* reveals Zola's profound ambivalence toward sexuality, but also reflects his pivotal place as a writer in the final third of the nineteenth century. No one saw this better than Maupassant, who rejects literary labels: "A son of Romanticism and a romantic himself in all his processes, [Zola] carries within a tendency toward poetry, a need to grow, to enlarge, to create symbols out of beings and things." This "tendency toward poetry" became clearer in some authors at the end of the century, turning the garden into a purely aesthetic motif, increasingly cut off from its narrative functions.

But before that, Madame de Mortsauf and Félix de Vandenesse, Julien Sorel and Madame de Rénal, Eugénie and Charles, Emma and Rodolphe, Marius and Cosette, Albine and Serge, had for decades made their mark on our imaginaries, turning the garden, with its bench and its shade, into the symbolic place of love—in the world and beyond it.

MARCEL PROUST, OR THE GARDEN RE-CREATED

One morning, while I was reading in the garden . . .

I was eighteen at the time, I had just finished reading *À la recherché du temps perdu* in its entirety on the beach of Sagres, in southern Portugal. The Algarve was still wild, the wind whipped the waves, the beaches were burning and deserted. We woke up to see the sun rise well before the hour when Marcel Proust would be going to bed. I hitchhiked back to Paris, then left right away for Illiers, which wasn't yet called Combray. The key to the "house of Aunt Léonie" could still be gotten from Monsieur Larcher who was the first to have the idea of turning it into a "writer's house." We entered through the garden. Monsieur Larcher spoke fluent Proust. His commentary was woven with passages from *Du côté de chez Swann;* it was seamless. I was enchanted, as if the text illustrated the house, and not the reverse. He pushed open the gate while saying: "A visit? Who can that be?" We entered the garden. That was my first shock. It was tiny. It was like going back to your school when you're an adult. The text was crafted too large for this minuscule space which my imagination had endowed with the proportions of a vast park. Without knowing it, I had just had my first Proustian experience: disappointment in the face of reality. I decided to disregard my impression. I had probably read the text badly, too quickly. At the end of the visit, I proudly signed the visitors' book: Bloch.

A reader of Proust constantly moves between two contradictory poles: the diktat of *Contre Sainte-Beuve,* which prohibits one from identifying the *me* who is writing with the *me* who is living, and the temptation to look in real life for tangible traces of the work. It is difficult to resist the need to believe, as proven by the existence of literary pilgrimages. Marcel Proust indulges in knowledgeable grafting in his work, and it is often fruitless to look for the original varieties. Yes, he was a magical gardener, able to transplant the most fragile species from one ground to another and make us discover, in their freshness, long-forgotten sensations . . .

And yet, it is difficult to imagine Proust gardening in "real life." At a very young age his asthma prevented him from being in the country, and we know that the mere smell of a plant could provoke an attack. But there are so many flowers and gardens in his work! All those lavish bouquets for the women he knew! Imaginary gardens, of course, but filtered through memory, watered by childhood memories, stays with friends, rides in carriages or cars: gardens that were henceforth forbidden, contemplated in his mind from the enclosed room where he wrote. Re-created gardens. Among the twenty or so passages devoted to this subject in *Du côté de chez Swann,* three represent key moments. In the gardens of Combray, of Tansonville, and of the Champs-Élysées the reader discovers the first signs of a unique sensibility to the world, to beauty, and to love.

The garden of Combray, an impeccable synthesis between his mother's and his father's families, is in fact the hybrid product of the Weils and the Prousts. How could I, during my first visit, have recognized the garden of Illiers there? It was inspired first by the country house in Auteuil of Marcel Proust's great-uncle, Louis Weil. That merchant, the brother of the father of Jeanne Proust, acquired the property in 1867. The village of Auteuil had just been connected to the commune of Paris. It preserved its country "feel," which had enchanted so many writers since the time of Boileau and Molière. Its proximity to the capital made it a desirable destination for Parisians. The 1,500-square-meter property, very long, goes from the rue Lafontaine to the rue de la Source, before it is intersected by avenue Mozart. Close to the rue Lafontaine (originally rue de la Fontaine, today rue Jean-de-La-Fontaine) is the rue Perchamps, which was reborn in Combray—so many bucolic names to which is added a rue George-Sand. All the elements for a coherent association were thus in place. The family went to Auteuil in the summer but also in the spring, or on the weekend when the weather was good. The entire Weil clan went there: the great-uncle, Louis Weil, a widower who liked pretty women, like Uncle Adolphe in *La Recherche,* the grandparents, Nathé and Adèle, the cousins and second cousins.

The incipit of *Jean Santeuil,* an unfinished, early novel which is clearly autobiographical, opens with a description of the garden of Éteuilles: "The little garden door closed slowly behind Jean who had returned a third time to say goodnight to his mother, and who had been rather badly received." From Auteuil to Éteuilles, the transposition is obvious. A closed door to open a novel? The Santeuils' garden is a closed universe, like the Eden to which it would be compared, as was Jean's childhood, as well. "You have a nice garden there, with a stream that looks pure," a visitor remarks. In fact, people went to Auteuil for the ferruginous water, as is indicated by the name rue de la Source. We find in *Jean Santeuil* a certain number of elements of the scenery picked up again in the description of Combray: "the loud sound of the fountain," "sixty treelike hawthorns that made a circle around the fountain," the scent of the rose bushes, the lilacs, the tall chestnut trees. Flowers give "to those who look at them an incredible happiness, the idea that the gardener was blessed, that the garden is a paradise." The almost childlike style of this passage contrasts with the much more subtle—and less paradisiacal—vision of the garden of Combray in *La Recherche.*

But this garden also borrows its traits, of course, from the "little garden" of Illiers, just as the entire village of Combray borrows from that town. The garden is located behind the house of Jules and Élisabeth Amiot, the sister of Adrien Proust, which became the "house of Aunt Léonie," after the character in *La Recherche.* As a rule, the Prousts would go to that town close to Chartres in the spring. But after the first signs of the nine-year-old Marcel's asthma, they stopped going there; the distant memory of it opened the door to transfiguration. Proust's work thus fuses different elements of the real, of memory, and of the imaginary.

A fence separates the garden of Combray from the outside world. On one side is the family, on the other, "strangers." They don't invite many people to visit; Charles Swann is one of the only exceptions. A few details highlight the intimate, a bit provincial, side of this garden: the iron table, the wicker chairs, the family gathered after dinner. The effect of being enclosed is further highlighted by two descriptions of sound: "the aggressive, shrill alarm bell" with a "ferruginous, unstoppable, icy" sound (three adjectives borrowed from the Auteil spring?) that is set off by those who live in the house, and the "double tinkling, timid, oval, and golden" of the bell reserved for visitors. At the beginning of *La Recherche* the Proustian style is apparent, with the use of zeugmas, which associate otherwise unrelated terms: here, a visual sensation (oval, golden) and an abstract, psychological term (timid) to describe a sound. This creates an effect not of preciousness but of precision in restoring a sensation unique to a synesthetic universe where "scents, colors, and sounds address each other."

That "double tinkling" announces the entrance onto the stage of one of the main characters: Charles Swann. It is also the opening of the drama of which Proust is the mischievous chronicler and which had already begun in the preceding pages. The family functions like any social group, with its types, its rituals, its roles, its exclusions. When faced with this visit, which was decided "on the spur of the moment," they play at acting natural: speaking loudly so as not to appear to be hiding anything, placing syrups on the table . . . This rapidly orchestrated scene follows the conventional rules of bourgeois politeness.

The only one who doesn't play by the rules is the grandmother. She distinguishes herself from the group with her sincerity, her whimsy, her goodness, her true feeling for nature.

She first appears "in the empty garden whipped by a downpour, pushing back her disheveled grey hair so her forehead could better enjoy the healthful wind and rain." She detests the artificial, overly symmetrical look of the garden, the work of the new gardener. She is distinguished by the generosity of her heart and her love of the beautiful, the simple, and the natural: she is an exception in *La Recherche.* For her, the garden is not just a simple, social decoration but a piece of nature. Sent like a girl guide to welcome Swann, she takes advantage "to surreptitiously remove in passing a few stakes from the rose bushes, so the roses would have a more natural look, like a mother who runs her hands through her son's hair, which the barber flattened too much, to make it puff out." In that tender gesture one sees a mother's taste for unaffected beauty, and in that of removing the stakes, the grandmother's discretely rebellious character vis-à-vis bourgeois conventions.

With the arrival of Swann several themes that are developed in the novel are introduced. First, there is the strictness of social rules, even in a bourgeois setting. Just as in the home of the duchesse de Guermantes, Charles Swann's wife, who is suspected of dubious morality, isn't welcome. Only the hero's mother goes to the trouble of asking after their daughter, Gilberte. Swann's property and the hawthorns on it are mentioned, but it is described somewhat vaguely as an estate from which he brings back peaches and raspberries.

The garden of Combray could just as well be a parlor. In it, the same blindness about the true personality of those whom one invites is apparent. This familiar Swann, whose family has been known for a long time, cannot be the figure who is received in the most exclusive salons of the Faubourg Saint-Germain. The son of a stockbroker (like the grandfather of the hero and the father of Jeanne Proust), he couldn't socialize with duchesses. Contempt and shortsightedness: "Our social personality is a creation of what others think. Even the very simple act that we call 'see a person whom we know' is in part an intellectual act." "That first Swann, completely at leisure, perfumed with the scent of the big chestnut tree, of the baskets of raspberries and a sprig of tarragon" is quite different from the one whom the hero meets later in the Guermantes' entourage, or from the man in love whom the reader discovers in *Un Amour de Swann*. With unparalleled subtlety and virtuosity Proust immerses us both in the past of the narrator, in the present of the characters, and in the future of the book.

There is no description of the garden itself, beyond the mention of a chestnut tree, flower beds, and roses. Only when the little room where the child goes to be alone appears is there any allusion to the scent of irises or of the wild black currants that grow against the window. As in Balzac or Flaubert, the garden is described less for itself than for the scene that unfolds in it with the arrival of Swann, on the evenings when he is invited to dinner. However, it is indeed an original garden, as *Jean Santeuil* suggests, and it is the setting for the novel's seminal scene: the mother's kiss.

Swann is an unintentional interloper. His presence at dinner deprives the child, who is sent to bed, of his mother's goodnight kiss. The child then experiences separation, the suffering of love, or rather, love as suffering, anguish, desire. As in the biblical garden, he disregards the parental prohibition and,

117

watching for Swann's departure, awaits his mother at the top of the stairs to beg for her kiss. The father, against all expectations, allows her to give in and to stay in their son's room, where she reads him *François le champi* by George Sand.

The gate that had opened to let Swann in initiated the slow process of the narrator's entire quest: "the re-creation through memory of impressions that are then deepened, clarified, transformed into the equivalents of knowing [. . .], one of the conditions, almost the very essence of a work of art . . ."

And so the door to the garden of Combray completes the cycle, it opens and closes the work itself, at the end of *Le Temps retrouvé:* "Everything had been decided at the moment when, no longer enduring the wait for the next day to place my lips on my mother's face, I had made my decision, I had jumped from my bed and gone, in my nightshirt, to stand at the window through which the moonlight shone until I had heard Monsieur Swann leave. My parents had accompanied him, I had heard the garden door open, ring, and close . . ."

Jules Amiot, Marcel Proust's uncle, was enthralled with horticulture. At Illiers he had created a garden, the Pré Catelan. This park on the edge of the Loir inspired Tansonville, Swann's property in Combray. During their strolls to Méséglise, "on the Swann side," the family had become used, since Swann's marriage to Odette de Crécy, to making a detour to avoid passing along the wall with the white gate covered with lilacs. But this day the Swanns are absent, so they decide to walk along the park . . . Though the lilacs are wilted, the path that climbs to the chateau is bordered with nasturtiums, and forget-me-nots, periwinkle, and purple and yellow gladiolas grow around the ornamental lake. A bit farther the hero, walking behind his father and grandfather, takes the little path that goes toward the meadow "pulsing with the scent of hawthorns."

In one of the most important scenes in the book, the child is transfixed by his ecstatic contemplation of the hawthorns. At a distance from the others, who are continuing their walk, he is alone, concentrated and completely absorbed in his observation. As Reynaldo Hahn describes Marcel Proust, during these "profound minutes" when "concentrating on a profound work of penetration and alternate aspiration [he] entered, so to speak, into a state of trance" (*Hommage à Marcel Proust,* 1 January 1923). But despite—or because of—his efforts, the narrator, who is still a child, fails to grasp, to put into words, that revelation at the moment when it happens. He experiences pure beauty, in particular in front of a pink hawthorn that represents its quintessence.

Only literary creation would enable him, much later, to transcribe and to capture the essence of that revelation as Proust does in that passage, joining the moment of the impression to that of restoration. Religious vocabulary (chapel, sanctuary, altar of the Virgin) expresses a sacred communion with the beauty of nature. We understand why those hawthorns give rise each year to a pilgrimage to Illiers/Combray, where there are readings that encourage the participation of fervent admirers of Proust.

The apparition of the hawthorn is immediately followed by another, but now of a profane and literary nature. In contrast to the garden of Combray, which is surrounded by walls, the park of Tansonville is visible from the exterior, from over the hedges. Beyond the hawthorn one sees flowers planted along the path: jasmines, pansies, verbena, gillyflowers, chosen for their fragrance and their colors. The delicate pink of "the deliciously blushing and Catholic bush" dedicated to Mary—thus to virginity and love—leads to the pink "as fragrant and faded as an old scrap of cordovan leather" of the gillyflowers, then to the green of the watering hose and its drops of multicolored water. The return to the profane is also seen in the accumulation of trivial objects connected to gardening: hose, spade, watering can.

The passage is composed like a painting: the setting is delimited by the hedge, the horizontality provided by the path, the diagonal by "the vertical and prismatic fan" of the water. Impressionism is often mentioned when discussing Proust. Granted, the scene could be a painting by Monet (*Jeune Fille dans le jardin de Giverny,* 1888, for example), provided that this essential fact is taken into account: Proust didn't paint from nature. All painting in his work is the work of recomposition, reconstruction, mental re-creation; it takes shape in the dark rooms of memory, intellect, the imaginary.

A young girl is suddenly standing in the garden in front of the young hero. The apparition provokes a true shock: "All of a sudden I stopped, I couldn't move," a moment parallel to the one when he came upon the hawthorns. Similarly, he is subsumed in the vision, "as happens when a vision doesn't simply address our sight but requires more profound perceptions and consumes our entire being." The parallel with the hawthorns is also created with colors: the girl's reddish blond hair, the pink spots on her face. That first look swallows all perception, drowns it, and operates a transmutation: the black of the eyes becomes dark blue, not really a color, but the sky blue of the gaze of the young boy who sees her. The force of the apparition, the first sign of love, already rests on a perception that is distorted by the effect of surprise, emotion, and subjectivity: "I didn't know then, and didn't learn later, how to reduce a strong impression to its objective elements." It is only a posteriori that the intellect can reorganize a vision. As often happens in Proust, the encounter was preceded and followed by a long reverie on the object of love. Gilberte is not a stranger to him: his imaginary had already seized onto her earlier, giving more strength to the encounter itself. The apparition is like the sudden materialization of his desire; the bedazzlement comes out of the wait.

What do we see of Gilberte herself? Her hair and her freckles, her black eyes that the young boy sees as blue. Nothing of her clothes, her size, her age, the shape of her face, everything that would have been described in detail by a nineteenth-century novelist. We see only her expression, indecipherable, and her "indecent" gesture, which isn't fully explained.

The scene is in fact suspended by the exchange of looks that follow, the look "that would like to touch, to bring the body he is looking at and its soul," of the boy, then the look that is sometimes contemptuous (in his opinion), and sometimes fixed but "without seeming to see me, without a distinct expression" of the young girl.

Then the voice of the mother of Gilberte, whose name is spoken only then, breaks the spell. With the return to reality, the different elements of the setting reappear: the spade, the jasmines, and the gillyflowers, the green watering can. As with the hawthorns, only creation can restore the essence of that scene. Scarcely perceived, Gilberte disappears, taking with her her fascinating mystery and, the hero laments, "the unknown of her life into which I will never enter." The essential mechanisms of Proustian love are in place: the disconnect between the intense desire of the one, and the indifference of the other, who is forever an enigma to the one who loves.

Gilberte goes to her mother, Odette Swann, and "a man dressed in twill" (we learn later that it is Charlus, mistaken for Odette's lover), the boy goes back to his father and grandfather. The hedge of hawthorns separates them; it is like a symbol or a prefiguration of all love in *La Recherche*.

Time goes by. A very heavy time, moving sometimes to the past with *Un Amour de Swann,* sometimes to an indefinite future with "Noms de pays," the final part of *Du côté de chez Swann.* The narrator is still rather young, because he still goes out under the supervision of the maid, Françoise, who came from Combray after the death of Aunt Léonie. His fragile health prevents him not only from traveling but from any situation that might upset him. Here he is confined to the Champs-Élysées, which awaken nothing in his imagination, a necessary condition for desire in him. The gardens of the Champs-Élysées are at that time both a place for walking, for pleasure, with the Café des Ambassadeurs and the Alcazar in the summer, and a playground for children. No, nothing in this public park connects him to his dreams: "Going to the Champs-Élysées was unbearable." The boy languishes, sitting next to the merry-go-round with Françoise.

Marcel Proust lived near there with his parents, on 9 boulevard Malesherbes. He had only to go down the rue Royale to get to the Place de la Concorde. He also went there with his friends from the Lycée Condorcet, Robert Dreyfus, Léon Brunschvicg, and Louis de la Salle. They met up with a "little group" of girls, including Antoinette Faure, the daughter of the future president of the Republic, Félix Faure, and Marie de Benardaky—the daughter of a Russian diplomat—with whom he was madly in love. In the dedication to *Du côté de chez Swann* he would write to Jacques de Lacretelle: "I thought for the scene of playing with Gilberte in the Champs-Élysées, in the snow, of a person who was the great love of my life without her ever knowing . . . Mademoiselle B*, today . . . Princesse Radzivill" (Jacques de Lacretelle, "Hommage à Marcel Proust").

The garden is described in its worst light: short and yellowed grass, a clump of linden trees against which Françoise places her chair. Neither the candy sellers nor the goat carts, not even the merry-go-round can distract that solitary, bored child sitting next to the basin presided over by a statue.

Then suddenly the name Gilberte, uttered in a clipped voice by a little girl picking up her racket and shuttlecock, comes through the air and renews the miracle of Tansonville. The wilted grass is transformed magically into "a marvelous little band the color of intangible heliotrope," while the red-headed Gilberte follows her governess, who is wearing a blue feather in her hat. The hero's life henceforth revolves around a single question: "Would Gilberte be coming to the Champs-Élysées today?"

Unlike the park of Tansonville, the public park, indeed because it is public, would enable the narrator to begin a relationship with Gilberte, and even to play *barres* with her and her friends. Proust's choice of that game is not insignificant: it consists of two opposing teams who must take each other prisoner. Could it be the image of his situation, a prisoner of his love for Gilberte when their families no longer spend time together? Or the image of a Swann, caught between the Verdurin clan and his frequenting the Faubourg Saint-Germain?

The boy soon discovers the modalities of nonreciprocal love, his passion encountering only the casual friendship of Gilberte. At the Champs-Élysées, as once between Swann and Odette, and as later between the hero and Albertine, love is born, lives, and suffers from the disconnect already analyzed by Proust in *L'Indifférent.* His encounters with Gilberte are subject to impediments that are beyond his control: the young girl's activities, outings, errands, mornings with her friends, and . . . the weather.

One winter day, for example, when Paris is covered with snow, he is allowed to go out thanks to an unexpected ray of sunshine. There are neither flowers nor scents in this evocation of the gardens. The frozen Seine is "caught like a huge beached whale," the merry-go-round doesn't move, the white lawns fixed in the black network of paths, a column of ice hangs from the statue. The Champs-Élysées are deserted. Marcel and Françoise wander like lost souls, frozen. This black-and-white scene is indeed evocative of impressionist paintings of Paris under the snow. However, for the boy, the landscape isn't perceived from an aesthetic point of view, rather as "the image of the powers that might prevent me from seeing Gilberte." Far from being sensitive to the magic of the sight, he, too, is caught in the ice.

The second apparition of the young girl is just as shocking as the first, although it is narrated with a touch of humor due to the disconnect between the concrete details (the circus, the puppet theater, the feather) and the hyperbolic vocabulary of the apparition: "All of a sudden the air rent apart: between the puppet theatre and the circus, on the embellished horizon, on the half-open sky, I had just noticed, like a fabulous sign, the blue feather of Mademoiselle." It was indeed a miracle, but it was announced by a sign that is banal, though infinitely desirable, as is all that touches the beloved object. Ah! If only Françoise had such a proud bearing . . . With the arrival of Gilberte, the static, black-and-white scene suddenly explodes with color, and begins to move. "And already Gilberte was running at top speed in my direction, sparkling and red under a bonnet trimmed in fur, animated by the cold, the delay, and the desire to play." A delicious irruption of the girl who glides like a skater "her arms wide open [. . .] smiling as if she had wanted to see me." An elegant image inspired in Marcel Proust by the Russo-Polish origin of the pretty Marie de Benardaky. "The headiness and the despair of [her] childhood"? (A contemporary of Proust pointed out that, when it turned cold, the Russian skaters went to the frozen lakes of the Bois de Boulogne). Gilberte and the hero are alone, as if it were the beginning of an intimacy. An old habituée of the garden witnesses their encounter and, like an ancient choir, celebrates Gilberte's vitality: "Brava! Brava!"

The gardens of the Champs-Élysées prefigure the outing to Balbec, where the hero, still suffering, would be fascinated by that same sporty vitality in the "young girls in flower." We often love that which escapes us, and it is just when we start to despair that the unhoped-for occurs: "That day brought progress to my happiness." The law of reversal that Charles Swann would not refute . . .

The so dreaded gardens of the Champs-Élysées ultimately provide the opportunity for the young boy to renew his acquaintance with Gilberte, who would be a faithful friend to the end of *La Recherche*. It is she who is chosen, by marrying Robert de Saint-Loup and through their daughter, to symbolically join together the Swann side and the Guermantes side. But those same gardens would also, more tragically, be the setting for the first signs of the stroke that would carry off the hero's adored grandmother. The first love, the first disappearance of a loved one . . .

In *Du côté des Guermantes,* concerning the character Françoise, Marcel Proust writes: "And thus it was she who was the first to give the idea that a person is not, as I had imagined, clear and immobile before us, with his merits, his defects, his plans, and his intentions with regard to us (like a garden, with all its flower beds, that we look at through a gate), but a shadow that we can never penetrate, of which there can never be direct knowledge, regarding which we form countless beliefs based on his words and even his actions, even though neither words nor actions can provide anything but insufficient and, moreover, contradictory information; a shadow in which we can alternately imagine, with just as much likelihood, that there burn equal degrees of hatred and love."

As an aside, in the image of a fence that frames and protects it, this comparison with a garden illustrates the incomplete, grid-like, flat perception of the human being whom we know only through our own projections, our own prejudices. Essentially, we never enter into the secret garden that is the "other," we never go through the gate. We perceive others only as "a shadow into which we can never penetrate." This is one of the great psychological and moral lessons of *La Recherche.*

Another lesson, at the very end of *Du côté de chez Swann,* is provided by the Bois de Boulogne, where the narrator, retracing his childhood steps, comes to understand "the paradox of seeking in reality the tableaux of one's memory, which will always lack the charm that comes from memory itself and from not having been perceived by the senses." This very beautiful passage is bathed in nostalgia, by definition "the pain of returning." Creations, the essence of which is ephemeral, gardens as "places we have known do not belong only to the world of space where we situate them for our convenience. They were but a thin slice in between the contiguous impressions that formed our life at the time; the memory of a certain image is but the regret for a certain moment in time; and houses, roads, avenues, are as fleeting, alas, as the years." Other gardens grow in *À la recherché du temps perdu,* such as that of la Raspelière, the Verdurins' property. But those of Combray, Tansonville, the Champs-Élysées (or the Bois de Boulogne, itself compared to a garden), share the privilege of being settings for revelatory apparitions. Swann, Gilberte, Odette—the three members of the same family—are the involuntary messengers of truths whose meanings appear only in Time.

Public Parks

Paris was one of the first cities to open royal gardens, such as the Palais Royal or the Tuileries, to the public, but it was Napoleon III who assigned the prefect of the Seine, Georges Eugène Haussmann, the task of transforming the capital. Four large parks: to the west, the Bois de Boulogne, a former royal estate; to the east, the Bois de Vincennes; to the north, the Parc des Buttes-Chaumont; and to the south, the Parc Montsouris. They all serve as the capital's green lung. They are also a way for the urban population to discover nature: one can admire waterfalls, row or skate on lakes, climb grottoes, have lunch in the shade: "One is no longer at the gates of a large city; one is in the solitude of the countryside," wrote Amédée Achard. In the city, twenty-four *places* which were turned into gardens on the model of English squares also enable Parisians to gather, and to strengthen social bonds with their neighbors while enjoying the fresh air.

The Tuileries, which were renovated by Le Nôtre, continued through the Champs-Élysées toward Versailles. The promenade was transformed into an English garden, and included new entertainment venues, such as the Alcazar, the Cirque d'été, the Carré Marigny, and the Musard concert hall.

ANDRÉ GIDE, LOVER
OF GARDENS

Nathanaël, I will tell you about the most
beautiful gardens I have ever seen.

—André Gide, *Les Nourritures terrestres*

Not many people know this, but of all French writers, Gide
was perhaps the one who was most smitten with gardens. Not
only does one encounter them everywhere in his writing, but
he himself was an experienced gardener, as seen in the many
notations in his *Journal.* The man who said, "Born in Paris
of a father from Uzès and a mother from Normandy, where,
Monsieur Barrès, would you like me to take root?," Gide never
stopped planting, though he never took root anywhere. But,
a man who enjoyed the moment, he entered completely into
the contemplation of the gardens he walked through, those
he sometimes possessed, then left behind, a man who planted
without always harvesting. Albert Camus insightfully notes in
"Rencontres avec André Gide": "Gide later reigned over my youth
and, to those whom you have admired at least once, how can
you not be forever grateful for having raised you up to that
highest level of your soul! With all of that, however, he was for
me neither a master of thought nor a master of writing. To me,
Gide was *the model of the artist,* the guardian, son of the king,

who guarded the doors of a garden where I wanted to live." A lovely image of a garden of delights where the young writer dreamed one day of entering . . .

Much more than Sartre or Camus, for me André Gide opened, if not the "gates of the garden," at least my eyes onto pleasures I didn't expect. I'm not talking about the homosexuality which my naïveté didn't even allow me to suspect, but a reversal of morality that enthralled me. "Gide is the one who gives the adolescent a certain amount of permission," notes Tiphaine Samoyault. *L'Immoraliste,* which I read when I was about fifteen, was a revelation. That asceticism in the conquest of the body and the construction of self, that celebration of life, had an incredibly tonic effect on my young girl's romanticism. I loved the vigor; I recognized myself in it.

It rained last night. The June wind pulls off the rose petals and shakes the leaves. The garden isn't as beautiful as it has been in the past few weeks, in spite of the hydrangea bushes in full bloom. A little garden in Île-de-France, with soil heavy when it rains and dry as brick when it's hot . . . Quite different from the vast Normandy properties where *La Porte étroite* or *L'Immoraliste* takes us. There are so many gardens in André Gide's writing that it would be a huge task to list them all. Whether they are in the form of a meager plot of grass or a few bushes, it is to those gardens that his gaze first goes.

He himself enjoyed several gardens, in La Roque-Baignard and Cuverville in Normandy, villa Montmorency in Paris, Cabris in Provence, in Les Audides at the home of Élisabeth van Rysselberghe, the mother of his daughter Catherine, or at

La Messuguière at the home of his friend Loup Mayrisch, not counting all those he admired here and there.

Thus, in the first paragraph of *Si le grain ne meurt,* an autobiographical text written when he was fifty-six, a garden is associated with his oldest memories: "I can see again the paper dragons, cut out by my father, which we would throw from the balcony, and which the wind would carry away, above the basin on the square, to the Jardin du Luxembourg where the high branches of the chestnut trees grabbed them." An aerial, light image, throughout a journey that flies above the rue de Médicis, in a connection between father and son to which death would put an end all too soon. Like Jean-Paul Sartre later, André Gide was an only son raised by his mother. Also like Sartre, he was taken to play in the Jardin du Luxembourg, where he kept apart from the other children. He even enjoyed trampling their sand castles as soon as his maid had turned her back. Self-indulgence or sincerity? In opposition to the stereotypes of his time about angelic childhood, he saw in himself only "shadow, ugliness, deviousness." The Jardin du Luxembourg would, however, be the theater for his awareness of the other, of difference, of unhappiness, of infirmity. André befriended an awkward boy whose last name was Mouton, then learned that he was becoming blind. The experience of loss as well, when one day Mouton stopped coming to the garden.

The Jardin du Luxembourg was indeed the place for a social education; a child would confront his peers, sometimes violently during fights between "aristos" from the Alsatian School, where he went, and students from the public school. Playing ball, fighting, but also, when he was older, carrying on long conversations with his friends, like Olivier Molinier and Bernard Profitendieu in *Les Faux-Monnayeurs*. There they discussed "art, philosophy, sports, politics, and literature." So many stages in that "learning about life" with his peers. Like Lucien, he was perhaps tempted to say: "What I would like is to tell the story not of a character but of a place—for example, a garden path, like this one, tell about what happens—from morning to night."

The Jardin du Luxembourg, like the streets nearby where he lived with his mother (rue Médicis, rue de Tournon, and a bit farther, rue de Commaille, where the houses opened onto hidden gardens), were the realm of the Left Bank bourgeoisie, a realm often inhabited at the time by academics and doctors. His father taught law at the university. Gide remained faithful to that garden, enjoying walking in it later in his life and meeting up with his writer friends, Pierre Louÿs or Paul Valéry.

Throughout his life Gide enjoyed visiting public gardens, which he preferred over "the most beautiful park enclosed by walls" (*Les Nouvelles Nourritures*). They offered the joy of contemplation or of conversation, as in the old days, while strolling: the springs in Uzès, the garden of la Fontaine in Nîmes, evoked in *Les Nourritures terrestres,* or the wonderful botanic garden of Montpellier, where he met with Paul Valéry.

Botany was, in fact, one of Gide's passions. In that respect he was a worthy successor of Jean-Jacques Rousseau and George Sand. When just a boy he was initiated into this science by the former governess and friend of his mother, the Scottish Anna Shackleton. He would never forget her and paid homage to her in *La Porte étroite* by including her under the name of Flora Ashburton. With humor and tenderness, in *Si le grain ne meurt* Gide describes the escapades of the "band of botanists" she belonged to. His mother encouraged the child to accompany them to get some exercise. Metal boxes hanging across their bodies, armed with pruning shears or sometimes a butterfly net, "old ladies" and "loveable maniacs" traveled the countryside to enrich their herbaria. Anna also took classes at a museum and gave full rein to her passion at the La Roque-Baignard property where the Gides spent their vacations. "At La Roque, the herbarium reigned as a lord; everything related to it, it was filled zealously, seriously, like a rite."

Anna instilled in André a taste for the natural sciences and for plants; she was also a confidant for him, a second mother. And so the plant world was associated with a protective and benevolent figure. This education through observation was all the more important because the schooling of the child was rather discontinuous owing to his fragile health. Nature and music, along with books, made up the essential part of his almost autodidactic training. Most of the time he took mediocre classes in private schools, like that of Monsieur Richard on rue Raynouard, where he also took his first steps in horticulture. He bought and planted a gladiolus bulb in a pot, which he claimed to see grow: "A green sprout had soon emerged out of the dirt, and its daily growth was marvelous." To record its growth, he noted its daily progress on a stick stuck in the pot. But, despite his efforts, he did not manage to *see* it grow. The pedagogical virtue of nature was no less important: "Ah! What a wonderful school is an orchard, a garden! And what a good teacher, often, one would make of a horticulturist!" he had Vincent say in *Les Faux-Monnayeurs,* an opinion that he obviously shared. He would rediscover that interest in botany much later, in Provence, with Élisabeth van Rysselberghe, a talented gardener and avid botanist.

The vacations of the young Gide were spent either in the region of Nîmes and Uzès (his father's side) or in Normandy (his mother's side) at La Roque-Baignard near Pont-l'Évêque. That huge 425-hectare property is evoked in *L'Immoraliste* under the name of La Morinière, as well as in *Si le grain ne meurt:* "The region not only lent me its setting; throughout the book I tried hard to paint a lifelike portrait of it." He met his cousins there, in particular Madeleine, who became his wife. The boys played their games in complete freedom. André read a lot, too, gathered plants, and fished for trout in the streams. Unlike the Jardin du Luxembourg, which was overly super-vised, La Roque was an enchanted territory around a fairy-tale castle, with its moats and its bridge, in the heart of the Normandy countryside. "How can you describe the delight a child feels living on an island, a tiny little island, which he can, moreover, escape whenever he wants?"

The enclosed space of the island opened onto the landscape, connecting constraint and freedom, two founding themes in the Gide imaginary. Water and plants, birds and fish, populate that kingdom without borders. What a disappointment when one day his mother showed him the actual borders on a re-gional land survey! "I don't really know anymore what I was imagining beyond the woods; and maybe I didn't imagine any-thing; but if I had imagined something, I would have liked to imagine it differently," the writer notes. This use of the verb "to imagine" four times tells us a lot about his need for the unknown and for adventure, which would continue throughout his life. It is thus a garden that extends over an entire region, without limits, that Gide draws, since the wall of the enclosure "allowed the gaze, looking above the barrier of the stream and beyond the garden, to plunge infinitely into the valley . . ." The memory of the adult encompasses the entire landscape within the enclosed space of the garden itself.

La Morinière in *L'Immoraliste* thus mirrors the property of La Roque, in the heart of the Auge region. The hero, Michel, lives there for some time as a gentleman farmer with Marceline, his wife, enjoying an orderly life after his revelation in North Africa following an adventurous existence centered around his own pleasure. Lush Normandy and its abundant water contrasts with the desert and the oasis of Biskra, sedentariness with nomadism, social norms with the affirmation of one's difference.

In *Si le grain ne meurt,* Gide also mentions Cuverville, the property of his cousin Madeleine, located some fifty kilometers from La Roque, in the Caux region. Purchased by their grandfather, Émile Rondeaux, it was bequeathed to Madeleine's father, Édouard Rondeaux. Gide lived there with his wife. "The garden of Cuverville, where I am writing this, hasn't changed very much. There is the roundabout surrounded by pruned yews, where we played in a pile of sand; not far, on 'the flower path,' is the place where we created our little gardens; in the shade of a silvery linden tree, the gymnastic stunts of which Emmanuèle [Madeleine] was so fearful, Suzanne, on the contrary, so bold; then a shadowy part, 'the dark path,' where on balmy evenings, after dinner, my uncle would hide; on other evenings, he would read out loud an endless novel by Walter Scott. [. . .] No, none of that has changed, and I discover deep down, without difficulty, the little boy that I was."

Like the estate of La Roque, Cuverville is full of memories. But while La Roque was sold in 1900, Madeleine continued to own Cuverville. The plaster on the house's façade was removed, returning the house to its original look, but the property still caused the lovers in *La Porte étroite* to dream, with its beech grove, its path edged with flowers, its dark path, and the little door at the back of the garden. Given the name Fongueusemare, it is the setting of the novel that was inspired, some twenty years later, by the tormented relationship between André Gide and Madeleine Rondeaux. The novelist worked "on the outline" there. He struggled between writing and gardening, as on 13 June 1905: "Since we've been here, the constant rain, ruining the garden, has actually helped my work. Every day I've been able to advance a few lines in my *Porte étroite*" (*Journal*). When the weather was good, the opposite was true: "All morning in the garden, I could not get myself to go inside and write. I arrived for lunch light-headed and Em. said I 'seemed obsessed.' Why would I appear so? Simply from looking for insects on my rose bushes" (May 1905).

The novel begins with an almost topographical description of the place. "The rectangular garden is enclosed by a wall. In front of the house, it consists of a rather large, shady lawn; one of its sand and gravel paths winds around it. On this side of the garden, the wall is lower and enables a view of the farmyard outside the garden; the farm, as is the custom of this region, is bordered by an avenue of beech trees." Unlike La Roque, enclosures dominate here: walls, the path, the farmyard, itself framed by the avenue of beech trees, form a quadruple enclosure. It is only behind the house that "the garden expands more comfortably." But there, too, walls and curtains of trees surround it. Only "a secret little door" enables one to join the copses and the avenue of beeches that surround it. However, from the front porch one's gaze can be lost over the distant countryside.

As suggested by the title, which is both literal and symbolic, and in a direct line from courtly literature, La Fongueusemare of *La Porte étroite* is an enclosed space, removed, and in a certain way, forbidden. The garden plays a major role in the novel. Following the rhythm of the seasons, key scenes play out in it up to the final encounter of Jérôme and Alissa at the end of the summer, on the threshold of the "narrow door." In spite of their love, Alissa abandons Jérôme definitively outside the garden and disappears after locking the little door. This not only descriptive but also diegetic function of the garden contributes to making *La Porte étroite* a novel of renunciation in the classical tradition of *La Princesse de Clèves* and the *Lys dans la vallée*.

After they were married, André Gide and Madeleine Rondeaux moved into Cuverville. The writer's *Journal* gives many examples of his passion for gardening. He orders flowers, fruit trees from the best nurseries, in France and abroad. "Hellebores, lilies, tigridias arrived from Holland. From seven in the morning to six in the evening I don't stop working in the garden" (March 1902). He adored pruning the rose bushes and the fruit trees, and quickly saw parallels between nature and art: "Mius is becoming talented in crossing some flowers; and I was finally able to convince him that in the beds of seedlings we are growing, the least robust varieties often produce the most beautiful flowers; but I have difficulty getting him to reject the common, hardy varieties which do without much care in favor of those that are more difficult to cultivate and demand more attention."

"If Greece counts no Lacedaemonian among its artists, isn't it because Sparta hastened the rejection of its sickly children?" (17 June 1910). In *Les Faux-Monnayeurs*, Vincent notes that "the buds that develop most naturally are always terminal buds— that is, those that are the farthest from the familial trunk." The same idea would recur in *Les Nouvelles Nourritures*. This is certainly not surprising from the one who wrote, "Families, I hate you!"

Gide's ambivalent relationship to Cuverville, his wife's estate which was often invaded by family and guests, led him to flee. During a trip to North Africa, first in Sousse in Tunisia then in Biskra, he discovered his homosexuality and his desire to be completely free. The closed universe of Cuverville, its narrow door, were counterbalanced by Gide's need for freedom, and conjugal love demolished by his desire for boys. North and South, winter and summer, rain and sun, constraint and freedom, compose a universe in which Gide's postulations are all entangled.

The initiatory experience of the journey to the south in the company of his friend, the painter Paul Albert Laurens, is found in several of Gide's books. The revelation of pleasure, of hedonism, of beauty, and of transgression gives rise to lyrical passages in *Les Nourritures terrestres,* in which several pages are devoted to gardens. "Blidah! Blidah! Flower of the Sahel! Little rose! [. . .] On the highest of their high branches, the unfettered eucalyptuses drop their old bark; it fell, used-up protection, like a coat that the sun renders useless, like my old morality that was useful only in winter."

L'Immoraliste also celebrates the sunny climate of the Mediterranean basin and its dissolving effect on "old morality" within the flame of sensations. In the public park in Biskra, "the sweet acacia whose flowers come very early, before the leaves, gave off their perfume, unless that sort of light odor came from everywhere, its source unknown, an odor that seemed to enter into me through several senses, and exalt me." It is in those gardens of Biskra and in contact with children that Michel's senses are gradually awakened. The Mediterranean gardens reflect his return to life, gardens like the Latomia dei Cappuccini in Syracuse, "where the lemons have the acidic sweetness of oranges," or like the plantings in the form of stairs in Ravello, attaching their vine branches under the azure sky . . .

The garden brings together all the potentialities dear to André Gide. Halfway between nature and culture, both foreign and protected, the garden is a concentrate of beauty and sensuality, whether it is a Normandy park shining green in the rain, or a rose garden, a palm grove, an Italian terrace garden, or an enclosed vegetable garden with a narrow door. The garden is even sometimes the only memory we have left of a lost time or place. "There are very small towns that have charming gardens; one forgets the town; one forgets its name; one wishes to revisit the garden, but no longer knows how to get there." But there's no nostalgia in Gide, I think. Gardens are in his image, "undulating and diverse," mirrors of a perpetual present.

THE THOUSAND AND ONE
GARDENS OF COLETTE

She wanted to have the world to herself, deserted, in the
form of a little enclosure with a trellis and a sloping roof.

—Colette, *La Naissance du jour*

Both masked and sincere, discreet and indiscreet, costumed
and offering her reader a mirror of incomparable truth, Colette is the quintessential creature of paradox. Sometimes the
woman gets on my nerves, but the writer always wins me over.
Because it takes just one page of Colette for me to slip into a
second skin, infinitely more comfortable than my own.

Her books have accompanied me during many of the stages
in my life. First, I was Claudine, enduring the collars of the
same name that my mother insisted I should wear. Lying on
my stomach in the grass or on the carpet in the sitting room,
I identified with that heroine who was my age, who, like me,
went to school, but who was so much bolder! I believed everything I read at that time. Claudine, like Jo in *Little Women,* at-
tracted me with her boyish allure. She escaped the rules imposed on girls. She was bold, original, unique. A rebel. Free.
Just like I wanted to be. Before Proust, Colette taught me about
the vagaries of love. She gradually sketched my image of the
future. I dreamed of having children, a garden, and of writing

books: I would be at the same time Sido and Colette—an ambitious plan! At thirty, I thought I was old. I was dragged out of adolescence kicking and screaming. To become an adult, as adults would say. I saw myself in *La Naissance du jour,* which Colette wrote when she was fifty. I applied that book of maturity and renunciation to my youth. I underlined passages in it with a purple pen and never went anywhere without my paperback copy covered with wrinkled red paper. I could have created my self-portrait at the time through quotes from it. And to say like Colette: "Do you imagine when reading me that I'm painting my portrait? Not at all! It's only a model . . ."

What I still love today is her insight, her intelligence about things and people, the enchantment of her language. Is she too much? Yes, sometimes. Her writing can seem overwritten, on the edge of preciousness, or marked by the excessiveness of her time. We write more soberly these days. More dryly. But where is the flavor? The flesh of the words? The sharp thinking that soars? The incessant work of her pen on blue paper?

She contributed greatly to the creation of her own legend: Colette and la Bourgogne, Colette and cats, Colette and Willy, Colette and her lovers, Colette and women, Colette and Sido, Colette at the Palais-Royal; she ultimately became a national monument. A member of the Académie Goncourt, commander of the Légion d'Honneur, she was given a state funeral. So French. So official. So far from the half-naked young woman who caused a scandal on the stage with her lover, Missy. She loved the theater. She was the actress of herself. Yes, Colette was the best role for Sidonie Gabrielle.

Critics and biographers have mentioned her multiple faces,

143

her "ambivalences and paradoxes": disguises, lies, scenarios, the construction of the myth . . .

Behind the clichés of the free woman, of the blossoming gardener, of the enrooted woman from Burgundy, of the naked dancer, of the sensual lover, another woman was in fact hiding. A nostalgia for childhood, the wounds of love, the pure and the impure, betrayals, losses: all in *La Femme cachée.* It was in the radiant transfiguration of her wounds and her trials that "the feminine genius" of Colette lived, as Julia Kristeva has demonstrated so well.

The garden was the place par excellence through which that complexity was expressed. Gardens are everywhere in Colette's writing; they are like projections of an interior space that is both real and imaginary from which she endlessly drew her inspiration. Of all my favorite authors, she is the one who was best able to live among gardens and to talk—and *write,* I should say—about them.

To love and to cultivate one's garden presupposes permanence, an enrooting in one place. There can be no garden without a span of time. Nature demands time, for birth, for growth, for development, maturity, for the end and for beginning again. It sometimes takes several decades for a tree to spread its branches and for the planted landscape to find its harmony. Nothing is ever definitive in it, but everything depends on the passing of time.

But Colette moved a lot, as she recalls with humor in *Trois, six, neuf.* But with each new home she made the place her own and, in a certain way, settled there "permanently." She was both sedentary and a nomad: a "seated vagabond" (*La Retraite sentimentale*).

With each new boyfriend or girlfriend there corresponded a new region, a new place to live, a new garden. "A woman claims as many homelands as she has had happy loves," Colette asserts, adding, it's true: "She is also born under each sky wherever she heals the pain of loving." If, with her loves and her second homes, she lived practically all over France, she had, from the age of eighteen, always had a home in Paris, on the Right Bank (the only two Left Bank addresses were Willy's). Beginning in 1938 she would live there permanently. I defend a Parisian Colette whose so carefully preserved Burgundy accent maintained the provincial legend. Even if, as she admitted, she always sought in the heart of the capital a province, *her* province.

Franche-Comté with Willy; Brittany with Missy, then Bertrand de Jouvenel; Corrèze with Henri de Jouvenel; Provence with Maurice Goudeket—these were her adopted lands, her homelands through marriage, in a certain sense. In those places she planted, maintained, or simply cherished gardens— they spoke to her of the garden of her childhood, the mother of all gardens, the cradle of her love of nature: the garden of her mother in Saint-Sauveur-en-Puisaye. The garden was lost very early on, following her family's ruin, but she turned it into the Eden of her memory, an original and literary garden. She describes it more specifically in two, rather late books: *La Maison de Claudine* (1922) and *Sido* (1929). These works introduce the development of the mythical figure of Sido, "a figure who gradually imposed herself on all of my work—my

145

mother." Sido had died ten years earlier, in 1912. From being an unknown, she became, under the pen of her daughter, a famous character.

The motif of the garden in Colette thus derives its source from the childhood home, even when it is inspired by later models. In that provincial setting one finds an association, without any blending, of the vegetable and the pleasure gardens, a shaded terrace and the orchard. In the garden there are eggplants and peppers, tomatoes, an apricot tree, lilacs, a walnut tree, wisteria, bignonia, 'Great Maiden's Blush' roses . . . Both so common, with its flower beds and gravel path, that it seems we have known it forever; but also so unique, a bit bohemian, with its decrepit arbor, its neglected lawn, its fence that is falling down under the invasion of the wisteria, as if absence and time had left their traces there . . .

La Maison de Claudine describes this double garden of Saint-Sauveur, "the Upper Garden" and the "Lower Garden," a dichotomy upon which the entire description in the chapter "Where Are the Children?" is based. There is a spatial opposition between the low and the high, the front and the back, but also a mental opposition between reality and idealized memory. Transfiguration only occurred after Sido's death. Images of the past become distant, are transformed, as if the real presence—even at a distance—of the real Sido had been a shield. She is mentioned only rarely in *La Maison de Claudine.* However, she is the one we hear, Sido, short and round under the wisteria, calling her children who are scattered in nature. The maternal garden is a lost paradise. It represents the place of lost innocence. It doesn't matter if it still exists, since "lost is the secret that opened—light, odors, the harmony of trees and birds, the sound of human voices that death has already suspended—a world of which I have ceased to be worthy? . . ." It exists only in memory, and only writing can resuscitate it. To the latent guilt from the fall there is thus added doubt: "Does what remains deserve to be depicted, with the help of poor words?" The very experience of writing is uncertain.

In its opening pages, *Sido* stresses the fundamental contrast between urban life and life in the provinces. Although raised in Brussels in a bohemian and intellectual milieu, Sido seems to find peace only in her house. She needs both those rare city escapes and the reassuring space of her garden that, in its very essence, comes out of the provincial land.

Colette would sing the praises of that mythology of the provinces, and would sometimes use it, along with Barrèsian accents of a celebration of the land and native roots. In the 24 May 1940 issue of *Marie-Claire,* wearing a "city suit" and beach sandals, the novelist invited photographers to Méré. She proclaimed: "That peasant whom I once was, how joyfully I envision becoming her again! A small house and a rather large garden are my ambition. There is nothing that cures the increasing neuritis of an old writer who scratches on paper better than scratching in the earth . . . And, to choose the pruning shears over the pen, I don't hesitate for a moment." A little white lie from the one who would never stop "scratching on paper"—but one that Pétainist propaganda wouldn't fail to make use of.

However, we must not forget Colette's passion for gardening:

it was authentic. A large number of examples of it are seen in her writing, even if she always employed gardeners, like that brown, curly-haired man from Provence, Étienne, to whom she pays homage in *"La Treille muscate."* He came every day, twice a day, as he recounted in his *Souvenirs*. "When she saw a catalogue, she wanted everything": roses, honeysuckle, morning glories, wisteria, anemones, which she was crazy about, zinnias . . . Insatiable Colette!

The most essential activities are found in her novels: seeding, digging, planting, or, as in *La Naissance du jour:* "After dinner, we mustn't forget to water the channels that surround the melons, and water by hand the balsam, phlox, dahlias, and the young orange trees whose roots aren't yet deep enough to drink alone from the earth, trees that aren't strong enough to become green without the help of the constant fire of the sky . . ."

Above all, it is in her garden that Sido is powerfully evoked in the work that bears her name. "I would have been happy to illustrate these pages with a photo," wrote Colette at the end of the chapter devoted to her mother. "But I would have needed a 'Sido' standing in the garden, amid the pump, the hydrangeas, the weeping willow, and the very old walnut tree." The garden was her empire. She stood "at the center of a bloom of gardens, winds, rays of sun" . . . The adult writer's gaze joins that of the child: Sido was an omniscient, all-powerful—probably too much so, sometimes—mother. She is described in the warm glow of the summer flowers, "because 'Sido' loved red and pink in the garden, the flaming shades of roses, lychnises, hydrangeas and torch lily, and even the winter cherry, although she claimed that its flower, pulpy and veined with red, reminded her of a fresh piece of veal . . ." She is the fixed point toward which everything converges, from which everything leaves—including the vagabond child, in love with the dawn and the awakenings in the "original, damp and confused blue." Sido senses what the weather will be, but also the mystery of a seedling that grows. She is the Pythia of the mysteries of the sky and the earth. The garden unfolds around her, it has meaning only in relation to her.

The garden is also, for that adopted provincial woman, a place of sociability, of exchange, of transparency, of conviviality: "Our gardens say everything." Over the dividing walls of the "backyard gardens," one exchanged advice, a plant, a string, a bouquet of violets, an indiscretion. An idealized view of a little town that was not always supportive of Colette's family . . .

And so the garden is halfway between the intimate, domestic, village space of the house and wild, open, expansive nature, a place of free exploration that one discovers by leaving the confines of the enclosed space. A child's freedom depends on "an easy scaling—of a fence, a wall, a sloping 'shed.'" That really does sum up Colette's life: a combination of freedom and chosen dependency, the life of the one who forever scaled walls to meet others or to return home; she was "both a homebody and a vagabond, like a cat."

Sido's key word is "watch." It was her first lesson, everything started with that. And throughout her life Colette would endeavor to follow that lesson, and she in turn makes us see. First, colors: blue and purple spring gardens, with their lilacs, violets, irises. But also, a burst of foxgloves, geraniums, zinnias, when summer brings them to life: "Pure red, a Chinese red, another saffron rose dominates" (*Prisons et paradis,* "La Treille muscate"). And what more can be said about the "ungraspable violet halo" that surrounds them in the light of Provence, or the "yellow light with red and violet shimmering" of the summers at Saint-Sauveur?

All the senses are called upon to speak of the marvels of the garden. The sand lily "raises up high, as quickly as it can, its rigid calyx, with its heavy perfume of a bruised peach." To see, but also to touch, smell, hear, and taste. "The wild onrush that in the summer rises from chlorophylls released by a storm, the iodine released at each low tide, the gust belched out by the vegetable garden that can no longer contain itself, or by the pile of refuse where black currant marc, picked fennel, and old dahlia bulbs ferment together; what incense for my independent and capricious nose . . ." (*Pour un herbier,* "Fétidité"). Relationships are woven between plants, animals, and humans. The garden is plants, but also creatures and men . . . A celebration of nature that is one and diverse! "So what did I want to tell you? That the peony has a scent, not of peonies nor of roses, but of cockchafers?" (*Pour un herbier*). Thus the imagination must relieve the senses in order to create poetry. How does one express the sumptuousness of nature? "Since we only have the word 'velvet' to describe velvet . . ." (*Pour un herbier*).

Colette indulges in the pleasure of words, of listing, of comparisons, of metaphors, of antitheses, but always with the goal of describing sensations most accurately, of keeping her descriptions as close as possible to reality. Like George Sand, she doesn't fear the "scholarly" word, but is careful not to use it only for itself. To see and make see. Feel and make feel. Always.

In the garden of *La Retraite sentimentale,* which depicts the very beloved estate of Monts-Boucons (under the name of Casamène) in the Jura, bought then resold by Willy, "the clematis rains down in purple stars," "the ivy is holding out a strong, twisted arm," the marigolds are as "round and gold as mandarin oranges," "the Indian marigolds, like hornets, in brown and yellow velvet, ruched with a little iron, hugged in its bursting calyx." The modest plants of the "destroyed and luxuriant" estate of Claudine, which blends with the memory, once again, of the childhood house and its two gardens. "If only I could wrap myself around it and its green garden like the walls of a well, like a wall that protects it from all eyes!"

The garden is living, and so it dies, it changes, it teaches modesty, resignation, even, because it enables the confrontation of two different times, that of nature and that of man. Like writing, it also imposes order. How does one find the right balance between too much and not enough, between the wild and the settled? Abundance and disorder can be fatal to it. The surge of lifeblood, the pulsing, the gushing forth must be domesticated, "cultivated" in the strict sense, both in writing and in gardening. Colette experiences this in her Provencal garden of "La Treille muscate," to which she devotes two texts in *Prisons et paradis.* In the first, the new owner launches enthusiastically into the adventure: "The garden, the garden; quick, the garden . . ." The disheveled vine, "vegetable blessings," rose bushes of every color; she fantasizes about a poetic garden. But, "Mad is she who dreams of disordered roses! Why not an English garden! I remember my plans as the heavy sins of knowledge." Because, she continues in the second text, "La Treille muscate 1930," a garden should adapt to the land, to the climate, to the path of the sun and the winds, and to the customs of those who have experience. Thanks to the gardener Étienne, she "now knows what a Provencal garden is: it is a garden that to surpass all others needs only to grow in Provence."

But the garden is also a privileged place of the emergence and the experiments of life. In its contained space, one can observe life, see its progress, celebrate its wealth: "Everything grows with divine haste: the lowest creature throws forth its greatest vertical effort." The power of nature is sung by a pantheist Colette. But that joy of contemplation is weakened in time, through the vital force itself. "Everything moves forward, and I remain. Don't I already derive more pleasure in comparing the spring that was than in greeting it when it arrives?" wonders the narrator of "Printemps passé" in *La Maison de Claudine,* as if it is an attention to the present moment, the only way to experience ecstasy, that is missing as one ages. A constant balancing act between attachment and dispossession . . .

Those two poles seem to me to be essential for an understanding of Colette. They can be traced back to the traumatic event of her childhood, when the house of Saint-Sauveur had to be relinquished, and all of Colette's possessions sold at auction. Along with the feeling of shame and uprooting there was that which resulted from Sido preferring her son Achille, the doctor, and happily moving to Châtillon, the village where he lived. Colette's life and work are marked by the need to possess then to leave before being dispossessed. In a certain sense, belonging is inseparable from dispossession, and it is loss, perhaps, that definitively creates a bond: "I belong to a land that I've left," writes Colette in *Les Vrilles de la vigne.* But do we need to possess a garden to love and describe it? "The land belongs to the one who stops for a moment, contemplates it, and moves on. The entire sun belongs to the naked lizard that warms himself in its rays" (*La Vagabonde*). Her last garden, that of the Palais Royal, although she could no longer move and had to be content with looking at it through the window, is the confirmation of this.

In *Les Vrilles de la vigne* she evokes a native land as a land of dreams. But "Jour gris" ends with this warning: "Don't go: you will look for it in vain." But, to look for that which has disappeared or exists only in one's imagination, that is the task of the artist. Memory and especially writing are there to restore what is both forever lost and forever restored.

Let's look at the very beginning of *La Naissance du jour:* "so here on earth does there exist a vegetable garden path where I can retrace my own steps? On the edge of a well, is that a maternal ghost, wearing a dress of old-fashioned blue sateen, filling watering cans?" The "vegetable garden path" returns her to her roots and, like her childhood wanderings, the path home leads her to Sido, to the source. And so Sido appears at the beginning of the novel as a tutelary goddess, always in her garden, associated with its attributes: the watering can, the pruning shears, and the wooden bucket. Her daughter finally understands the

153

lesson: "She knew that we possess by abstaining, only by abstaining." That apology for renunciation—which is an acceptance of age, of time—would the narrator be able to apply it? Sido gives her a mission, that of "pursuing what as a poet she grasps and abandons, as one grasps a fragment of a floating melody" . . . To grasp and to abandon, always a dual movement. It is again the garden that offers the key to that mission: "She wanted the world to herself, deserted, under the vault of a little enclosure, with an arbor and a sloping roof."

The secret of the quest was already presented in *Sido*. In the modest setting of a walled garden with its pots where seeds are stored, a mother teaches her daughter to respect the mystery of that which grows under the earth—even if she already knows that it is a wasted effort. She assumes that the child won't be able to resist the desire to see what is hidden under the earth, that she is already possessed by "the solitary obsession of the treasure hunter."

And so the garden is not just an enchanted place of childhood memories, nor a place to work on a descriptive style. It is the paradigm of a life of writing: "What is most important is that I reveal and raise up into the daylight that which the human eye hasn't, before my own, yet touched" (*Sido*). To scratch the earth, to scratch the paper, the metaphor makes sense in the end. Like Claudine in *La Retraite sentimentale,* one must "scratch the humid earth" to bring forth the first throatful that tastes of the stone and rust . . . In *La Naissance du jour,* digging around then mulching the mandarin trees reflects the same fascination: "Seeing what lies beneath the earth renders attentive and avid all those who live above." There is creation

154

only with that curiosity about what lies below, about the buried treasure.

The garden teaches us something else: "Gardening connects the eyes and the mind to the earth, and I feel love for the happy aspect, the expression of a rescued shrub, nourished, supported, cared-for in its straw, covered with new earth . . ." The maternal care of the creator for her creation, the flood of love that is borne toward that which seeks to be born and to grow: once again, Sido isn't far away, she who left her daughter to wander in the blue dawn because she had confidence in her. The garden teaches us that all life comes out of a multitude of new beginnings, of little deaths and resurrections: "To wipe the slate clean, to rebuild, to be reborn, that has never been beyond my abilities," says the narrator of *La Naissance du jour.*

The garden in Colette's work is thus much more than a garden; rather, it is not just a garden. It is the place of the eternal return, of rebirth, of roots, in the literal sense, of creation and of life. From the flowers of Saint-Saveur to the elaborate beds of the Palais-Royal, from *Claudine* to *Paris de ma fenêtre* gardens constitute the fertile earth of Colette's work, and her essential loving and tormented loyalty to Sido, eternally at the heart of her compass rose. Simone de Beauvoir describes Colette in *La Force des choses:* "Paralyzed, her hair disheveled, violently made up, age gave her sharp face, her blue eyes, a brilliant shine: between her collection of paperweights and the gardens framed by her window, she looked to me, immobile and regal, like a formidable goddess-mother."

JEAN-PAUL AND SIMONE IN THE JARDIN DU LUXEMBOURG

The Luxembourg adorned with big yellow and purple irises.

—Simone de Beauvoir

Legend has them sitting in the cafés of Saint-Germain-des Prés, where an intersection bears their names, or in Montparnasse where they are resting together in the cemetery. They never owned a garden, not even a house, preferring hotel rooms, then, when they became known, modest apartments. They traveled the world, but they always lived within the confines of a single neighborhood. "If I consider the path of my life," wrote Simone de Beauvoir in the final volume of her *Mémoires,* "it is striking in its continuity. I was born in Paris, I lived in Paris [. . .]. Today I live five minutes from the place where I first lived" (*Tout compte fait*).

Sartre, whose *Les Mots* perhaps owes something to Beauvoir's autobiographical undertaking, for his part states: "I began my life as I will probably end it: in the midst of books." The same sense of unity, but for him, intellect is substituted for space. Reading and writing: *Les Mots* revolves around that axis, a true spine that holds the man Sartre up.

As opposed to Gide, nature was not part of Sartre's life experience: "Lush memories and the sweet folly of a peasant childhood, I would seek them in vain in myself. I never dug in the earth or looked for birds' nests, I didn't collect plants or throw stones at birds. But books were my birds and my nests, my pets, my barn, and my countryside." He stresses how different his life was, at a time when boys received training in the country, learned how to hunt and fish, "virile" activities, to shape a spirit of adventure and to conquer the real. He grew up away from the earth, had no tactile grasp of the world; that was replaced by books. His universe was the product of a true reversal, where abstraction was considered reality. Books didn't create a screen between him and the world; they *were* the world, and words "the humus of [his] memory." "In them," he adds, "I found real birds, in them I hunted true butterflies resting on true flowers."

And so reality, the Jardin d'Acclimatation or the Luxembourg, could offer only an imperfect version of the nature he first encountered in books, a nature that was described, classified, considered, assimilated. An imperfect copy. The location of the family apartment further accentuated this distance from the real. "A sixth-floor Parisian apartment with a view over roofs" was his "natural place." Sartre saw the world from on high, from afar.

Although both Sartre's and Beauvoir's families were from the provinces, their universe was indeed urban, Parisian, "a decor planted with the hand of man" (*Mémoires d'une jeune fille rangée*). As children, Sartre lived at 1, rue Le Goff, and Beauvoir at 103, boulevard du Montparnasse, then rue de Rennes. But for these early twentieth-century children, the street was only a place of passage under escort; it was most often from the window that they contemplated it. The pavement was still the domain of the kids of the people, Gavroche or Poulbot. Only they played in the street or on the sidewalks, running around freely. The children of the bourgeoisie went to the park under the surveillance of their nanny or their maid.

Jean-Paul was taken to the Luxembourg every day by his mother. They lived just a short walk away from the main entrance. In *Les Mots,* he paints a harsh, albeit stylized, portrait of the child he was then. An only child, without a father, he grew up spoiled, adored by his grandfather with whom he and his mother lived. He played the role they wanted him to play: precocious child, the little genius who would have a great future. He didn't go to school, so was never confronted with children his own age. He was the hero of the family play, "flying from imposture to imposture."

Like André Gide, it was in the Luxembourg that he was exposed to and interacted for the first time with his peers. From the perspective of an adult, he expresses the same disdainful judgment of the child he was at the time. But his experience was even more bitter because, unlike Gide, he had no direct contact with others. That would occur only later, in La Rochelle when his mother remarried. In contrast to his hyperbolic admiration for the other boys, who were described as "strong, fast, handsome," "flesh and blood heroes," Sartre expresses irony when he describes himself. Anything that was unique or extraordinary in him disappeared, "neither a marvel nor a monster," he endured the worst fate for a child who grew up under the adoring gaze of his family: his peers didn't see him. Worse than hell. That indifference annihilated him, relegated him to nothingness.

It also led him, if we believe *Les Mots,* to become aware of his being short, of being ugly. His mother infantilized him and, without meaning to, humiliated him even more by proposing to act as intermediary between the mothers of the other children ("the women who sat knitting on the iron chairs") and him. In the face of her failure, in the end it was still just the two of them: "We would go from tree to tree and from group to group, always imploring, always excluded."

And so the Jardin du Luxembourg wasn't an evocative or nostalgic place of happy memories. Sartre never mentions the trees, the flower beds, the statues, the pools. It is the setting for his revelation about his relationship with others, and about the lie in which he lived. An abstract setting, empty of any feeling for nature, scents, sounds. It was a trial of truth that could have played out in a school playground, for example, if he had lived a less protected life. When he compared himself to other children he always fell short: "I had seen the heroes running and fighting in the Luxembourg; stricken by their beauty, I understood that I belonged to an inferior species." A harsh judgment that contained an essential element: the awareness of his physical smallness and his ugliness which forced him to give up his dreams of becoming a fighter. In this world of boys, strength, height, aggressiveness, were the essential qualities. "I had to give up on myself." It is no coincidence that this text is situated between "Lire" and "Écrire," the two parts of

Les Mots. This renunciation would lead him to his destiny as a writer. Writing would become a form of compensation.

Sartre's ideal of being an upholder of right returned, however, in a recurrent dream, whose setting was the Luxembourg where he had to protect a little girl from death. But "Poulou" had to wait to grow older before finally making friends, and even to fight, he, the one who was "excluded from the public parks." He lived to write: "It's my habit, and my profession." *Les Mots* gives an elaborated shape to what was probably a more diffuse feeling and a more complex reality, if we are to believe his *Entretiens* with Simone de Beauvoir: "I had a puppet theater made up of piles of little characters into which I slipped my hands; I brought it to the Luxembourg, [. . .] I went behind a chair and imagined a stage where I made my characters act." A show that enthralled the little girls, his first admirers. The one who was "excluded from the parks" was already a seducer.

One might think that the public park described in *La Nausée* is more powerfully evocative: the black root of the tree that Roquentin is looking at, the sparse grass of the lawn, "the happy gurgling of a fountain, vital odors, little heat clouds floating in the cold air." Sartre even observed the tree before writing, like Maupassant on the advice of Flaubert. A professor at Le Havre, in October 1931 Sartre described it to Simone de Beauvoir to learn its name: "You know, those toys that spin in the wind or when you wind them up tightly; there were tiny green twigs frolicking around with six or seven leaves holding on, let's say, just like this." And he drew it. A chestnut tree, responded the "Beaver." The drawing probably didn't really do it justice. The park services in Le Havre were clear: there were no chestnut trees on the Saint-Roch square before the war, as Philippe Lançon notes. Maybe it was a maple tree? Would the face of philosophy have changed because of it?

In any event, it wasn't leaves or branches that captivated the attention of Sartre/Roquentin, but the root and the trunk: "A reddish green covered it up to the middle; the bark, black and blistering, looked like boiled leather." The tree he describes refers, of course, to himself. It's not symbolic, not a source of pleasure or lyricism, it is pure existence. Roquentin's experience with the tree is only a stage in his philosophical awareness of contingency and the absurd. The chestnut tree remains an abstraction, a philosophical object, just like "that plane tree, with its patches of decay, that half-rotten oak tree" in which Gaston Bachelard, in *La Terre et les rêveries du repos,* saw "the displacement of the normal image, of the verticalizing archetype."

In *L'Enfance d'un chef,* the chestnut tree (again!) would be assigned even more radically to its ontological condition as thing, without awareness or any possibility of dialogue. "He said 'chestnut tree!' and he waited. But nothing happened. [. . .] When he said: chestnut tree, nothing happened at all. He muttered under his breath: 'Rotten tree'; he wasn't reassured, but since the tree didn't move, he repeated more loudly: 'Rotten tree, rotten chestnut tree! Just wait, just you wait!' And he kicked it. But the tree remained calm, calm — as if it were made of wood. [. . .] Things, it was stupid, they didn't really exist."

Sartre's relationship with nature was actually almost phobic. For example, again in *La Nausée,* there is the vision of a

161

proliferating, invasive, monstrous octopus-like vegetation. "The Vegetation climbed for kilometers toward the towns. It waits. When the town is dead Vegetation will invade it, it will climb on the stones, it will hug them, dig around them, make them burst with its long, black claws; it will fill the holes and allow its green paws to hang everywhere" (*La Nausée*). No doubt, Sartre "was allergic to chlorophyll," as Simone de Beauvoir would sum him up.

Things were quite different for her. Her first steps as a child in Paris also led her to the Luxembourg. It was like a hyphen between them. Sartre entered by the front entrance, she from the back. They may even have crossed paths there, Poulou holding onto his mother's hand, Simone skipping in front of her maid Louise, with her bucket and shovel. The well-bred little girl made sand castles, played with her dolls. But there was no question of playing with an unknown child. Her mother would never have allowed it.

The Luxembourg, "with its untouchable flower beds, forbidden lawns," was for Simone a playground, enclosed by strict rules. It was also the theater of shocking temper tantrums by that model little girl. They occurred each time she was confronted with "the arbitrariness of prohibitions," when the principle of reality contrasted with the principle of pleasure: for example, when she had to leave the park where she was playing to go back home. "I screamed so loudly, for so long, that people in the Luxembourg sometimes thought I was being abused. 'Poor little thing!' said a lady, offering me a piece of candy.

I thanked her with a kick." The violence, the antisocial nature of her reactions, contrasted with the cocoon of bourgeois upbringing woven around her. Her tantrums became so famous in the family that one of her aunts wrote a fictional tale about them. Simone saw the distortion between the scene as she had lived it and the story that was told about it. "That day I suspected that literature had only an uncertain relationship with truth": the opposite of the conclusion of the child Sartre, for whom truth was in books. The intuition of the fictional nature of literature thus existed early on, which did not at all prevent Simone de Beauvoir from sometimes using it, including in her *Mémoires*.

Her violent moments were also signs of rebellion against the world of adults, social rules, the constraint they sought to impose on her—"a fiery vitality" and a radicalism, an extremism, a taste for the absolute that would never abandon her; it was a position that was very different from that of the little Jean-Paul, who sought on the contrary to be the ideal child for the adults who surrounded him.

Later, the Luxembourg would be her favorite place for walking, for reading, and for conversations with friends. It was the counterpoint to the family apartment, far from the maternal gaze and the rigid obligations to which girls were subjected. She studied for her *bac* seated on the edge of the Médicis fountain, in the sun, or in the English gardens. She read there, played the young emancipated girl. A few years later, she dreamed of her life while reading about that of Isadora Duncan. But Simone's ideal was modest. "I only wanted love, to write good books, to have a few children." In the Luxembourg, she met René Maheu (Herbaud in the *Mémoires d'une jeune fille rangée*), with whom she fell in love, and who was with Sartre at the time. She would only really get to know Sartre later, when she was working on a degree in philosophy. The Luxembourg was then "adorned with large yellow and purple irises." How many young girls of my generation or of the preceding one dreamed of that encounter, recognized themselves in Simone's childhood, identified with her life, were carried away by her example! Not everything was true? The essential was there, and that was enough. Simone de Beauvoir was the first writer to allow me to imagine that I could be one, too.

Her ties with Jean-Paul Sartre were formed during her preparation for her oral exam. Their connection would be sealed during a vacation in the Limousin. He met up with her on the sly, she ran across the park of the family property to join him. How romantic! Back in Paris, in September, they would meet in the morning "in the grey and golden Luxembourg, under the white gaze of the stone queens" (*La Force de l'âge*). They would never again be separated. How could I, or thousands of other well-bred young girls, not have dreamed that I, at the same age, would one day meet my own Jean-Paul Sartre? But that's another story . . .

Simone de Beauvoir's true paradise was Meyrignac, near Uzerche in the Limousin. Her description of the summers spent on her father's family property differs from the overall tone of *Mémoires d'une jeune fille rangée*. "Everything changed when I left the city and was transported among the animals and plants, into nature with its countless wonders." Meyrignac, or paradise lost. I visited the estate some dozen or so years ago, accompanied by a distant cousin of Simone de Beauvoir. "I couldn't imagine," Simone wrote, "that there existed on earth a more pleasant place to live." One can easily believe her.

Her grandfather's presence dominates her description. The former bureaucrat at the Paris *mairie,* a gardening enthusiast, designed a one-hectare landscape park in the middle of an eighty-hectare estate. At his side, Simone learned the names of trees, flowers, birds. Her excellent memory recorded them, even though she hadn't returned to Meyrignac in ages: "cedars, giant sequoias, purple beeches, Japanese dwarf trees, weeping willows, magnolias, araucarias"—they were all engraved in her memory forever. A beech tree with fernlike leaves, a catalpa under which she worked on the sacrosanct vacation homework. The English river, "dammed for artificial waterfalls, blooming with water lilies," still winds around the little island. But what Simone de Beauvoir remembered above all was the freedom she enjoyed while exploring the countryside. Like the Colette of *Sido,* she got up at dawn to surprise the sleepy land. "I was the only one who was carrying the beauty of the world." In a beautiful, lyrical passage, she describes her discovery of nature. "I learned of the buttercups and clover, the sugar phlox, the florescent blue of the morning glory, the butterfly, the ladybug, the glow worm, the dew drop, the spider webs, and gossamer . . ." Quite far from Sartrean intellectualism, Simone de Beauvoir preferred the side of sentient memory rather than analysis; the pleasure of words for their evocative power, words that she strives to restore as closely as possible to their source. Olfactory and auditory sensations played a large part: "The buzzing of the wasps, the squawking of the guinea fowl, the anguished call of the peacocks, the murmuring of the leaves; the scent of the phlox mixed with the smell of caramel and chocolate that reached me in clouds from the kitchen. [. . .] Every thing and myself had our place right here, now, and forever."

In these Limousin pages of *Mémoires d'une jeune fille rangée* we discover a Simone de Beauvoir who is very different from how she is usually perceived. The garden of Meyrignac, half park, half countryside, contains treasures: a love of nature, sensuality, gourmandise, a love of life, a feeling of fullness, a need for freedom—all made their nests there. In the garden, she later learned to enrich her human experience, to seek in nature the meaning of her own life, and in the infinite variations of the landscape the presence of a God in whom she still believed. Her exaltation was limitless, she gave herself up to the joys of contemplation, drunk on freedom. It was at Meyrignac, as well, that she would have the revelation of the metaphysical void that filled her with anguish; fundamental, existential experiences that only the freedom and solitude of the large estate could provide her.

Speaking of the Sartre-Beauvoir couple, she wrote in *La Force de l'âge:* "His mandate was to bear witness to all things, and to assume responsibility for them in the light of necessity; mine was to lend my awareness of the multiple splendors of life, and I would write in order to pull him out of time and nothingness." She had seen the first signs of those "multiple splendors" in the park of the Meyrignac property. It is that sense of abundance, her love of life, the gift of happiness, that

I love above all in Simone de Beauvoir. I believe that if she, like George Sand or Colette, influenced generations of women, it is *also* because of her ability to grasp a shimmering reality, and to reconstruct it in a unique, singular, liberated, yet very reflective, accessible, way.

ENTIRE DAYS IN THE PARK
WITH MARGUERITE DURAS

We had a park right out of a novel.

She doesn't use the word "garden," or only rarely. She uses "park," even when she's talking about a garden. Marguerite Duras's garden is above all that: a park. Bigger, more noble, etymologically: enclosed grounds that surround a chateau. The effect is one of amplification, of dramatization. In a garden, one gardens. In a park, one strolls. In Duras's park, roses are wild, and the paths, the beds, the grass, the stone basins, the linden trees, seem to have been there for all of eternity. The house—a chateau or a large manor in the reader's imaginary— has a terrace; the terrace looks out over the park, the park over the forest; one's gaze is lost over the horizon. One walks on the paths, one sits on a bench or rests on a chaise longue, one contemplates the mist that descends over the river or pond, the dusk that darkens the colors. The landscape is waiting. Often, one looks at the park from the house, through a window or a glass door. The window frames it like a moving picture or a film shot. Climbing plants, preferably rose geraniums, compose a vegetal screen that mirrors the exterior setting. In the house, bouquets of wilted flowers, rose petals, and dried lavender suspend time. The park opens up at the foot of the house;

its boundaries are uncertain; it enters the room by way of the plants on the windowsill, and continues toward the trees of the forest. It belongs to the intimacy of the house, but also to the wildness, to the unknown, to the violence of the forest. "The park is the entrance to the forest."

I must confess, it took me a long time to like Marguerite Duras. I use the word "like" on purpose. I didn't *like* her. Not her books, not her writing, not her films, and even less, her plays. And most of all, her as a person. And the more she was adored, the less I liked her. Her simplicity: affected. Her famous style: affected. Her female characters: affected. I saw only artifice in her, a coquetry that was all the more affected since it assumed the form of privation. All was lies, fabrication. And yet, everything should have conspired to make me appreciate her—what do I mean? . . . adore her!: my generation, feminism, my culture, my taste for Robbe-Grillet, Butor, Beckett, etc. And it wasn't for lack of trying, either: the almost empty Théâtre Récamier, where a dozen audience members tried to keep the flame alive, the applause at the end sounding gloomy; reading and rereading her novels; a somnambulistic viewing of her films. Something in me resisted. The worst was when the media embraced her, when she became the arbiter of the contemporary world and bestowed her peremptory judgments on everything and on nothing. This Duras cult exasperated me. And then, time passed. The little woman with the head of a frog died. I read her works again, persuaded that they must be hiding something that escaped me before. One must never give up on liking, seeing. Yes, there are still lies, fabrication, arrangements with the truth. Yes, she often imitates herself. No, not everything is interesting. But now I saw that Duras was a great writer. It's not she who had changed; rather, it was I.

One of Marguerite Duras's earliest texts is called *Un Parc de roman.* It dates from the beginning of the 1940s, when she had not yet published or even written a novel. It is the starting point of her literary work, the first thing she wanted to write, carefully, almost academically, the way one transforms a memory, an emotion, into sentences. She even turned it explicitly into a *literary object,* a park midway between reality and fiction, as we find in Gérard de Nerval or Alain-Fournier. "We had a park right out of a novel. We knew it very well, and yet we were able to lose ourselves in it, like in a forest. For me, that park always had the hue of the past: scarcely were we in it than we knew we had to leave." It was its future absence that gave it its worth, conferred its literary color on it. That familiar and mysterious place with "large spaces filled with humid shade," is one of melancholy, abandonment, solitude. All the elements of the Duras landscape can already be found here: the little oval pool surrounded by ivy, the paths, the old porch, the tall trees, and even the "wild and thorny roses that seem to be poisoned with a purple red." This Sleeping Beauty park is the cradle of Marguerite Duras's early literary endeavors — *La Famille Taneran,* which would give birth to the novel *Les Impudents,* and to a certain degree to her second novel, *La Vie tranquille.*

After that time, the luxuriant vegetation of Asia connected to the mother in *Un Barrage contre le Pacifique* and much later in *L'Amant* invaded everything. One almost forgets that, at the very beginning, there had been that park and that house, on her father's side. "The literary park" is somewhat the prehistory of the writer Duras.

Her father, Henri Donnadieu, bought Le Platier in 1921 in Pardaillan, in his native region, the Lot-et-Garonne. The little town of Duras was only a few kilometers away. The landscape had smaller hills, was more pleasant than the Haut-Quercy in which Marguerite would place Le Platier in her novel *Les Impudents;* it was also different from the Entre-deux-Mers in which she places it in *L'Amant.* Ill, suffering from the aftermath of dysentery, Henri Donnadieu was forced to leave his wife, Marie Legrand, and their three children, who remained in Indochina. The bill of sale, which includes the house—the home of a master with the feeling of a monastery—also lists the dependencies, vegetable and pleasure gardens, the workable land, fields, vineyards . . . "It wasn't a chateau, it was a house of rich wine makers, with a cellar as big as the house, wine, plums, and lots of vines," Marguerite Duras would comment. In the center of the park, which was actually a pleasure garden, between the house and the road, there were tall pines and an oval pool with goldfish, and boxwood hedges surrounding flower beds.

Henri Donnadieu would live only two months at Le Platier before he died, on 4 December 1921. Marguerite was seven years old. After a long journey, the mother and children in turn arrived at Le Platier. The house had been closed for six months; the family nevertheless moved in, and Marguerite discovered the park, the hills, the river, the sweetness of the landscape, the seamless passing of the seasons. She gathered up images, sensations, experiences, including solitude. "The great leap of my childhood into the unknown, was while my brothers were at the priest's learning Latin, *my entire days in the park*. Alone" (*Libération,* 27 February 1992).

Two years later, Marie Donnadieu, her two sons, and her daughter went back to Phnom Penh. When they returned to France in April 1931, the house, which had been unoccupied since they left, proved to be uninhabitable. The park was overgrown, the greenhouses falling down, the vines untended. The Donnadieus had to seek the hospitality of neighbors. Marie decided to sell the property, the only link that connected her to her husband, to the father of her children. It was done on 19 May 1931. "One day, we will put everything right," the narrator of *Un Parc de roman* promises herself. In fact, up until her death, Marguerite never stopped wanting to buy back that property, which was even more run-down, and bring it back to life. In vain.

When she published her first novel, *Les Impudents,* she chose to do it under the pseudonym Duras. Enough has been written on this abandonment of her father's name. Except that it really wasn't an abandonment, since she adopted the name of the town next to Le Platier, Duras, in the land of her father. To situate herself in the world as a writer, she broke with her social identity (for the orphan, her mother's married name) and quite naturally drew from the source of her inspiration, the site of her first attempts at literature. Duras, the name of a place, was rooted in the paternal land. From her absent, forgotten father, who in fact doesn't appear in her work, she doesn't create a character more important than her mother, but she appropriates his origins, makes them her own. Gradually, her first name would slide away and disappear. Only Duras would remain.

Le Platier thus became Uderan in *Les Impudents.* The heroine, Maud, chooses to sleep there in spite of the decrepitude of the place. Returning home one night, she goes through the silent park. The mystery that emerges from the giant boxwoods and pine trees reassures her. In the daylight, in the company of her mother, she witnesses the arrival of the handsome Georges Durieux. The paths, the linden and pine trees, even the wild roses that turn violet in the dusk, all the elements of the "literary park" are found here. But the young novelist gives them a more dramatic touch, "surrounding the flower beds, there awakens a blood-red color." The weight of waiting and of boredom that stifles Maud also weighs on the setting, in a very Mauriac-like ambiance. As in Duras's real life, the park and the house will be sold by the heroine's mother.

In *La Vie tranquille,* Duras's second novel, which was more successful in spite of some tedious passages (years later she would consider it "magnificent"), the estate and its park appear again, even if the "earthy" touches are more accentuated. But, this time, the narrator specifies that no one dares go into the wild park. It remains a mysterious, almost forbidden place.

The key to these recurrent images is perhaps provided in a handwritten text dating from the beginning of the 1940s. In it, Marguerite Duras gives a literary version of the last moments of her father's life, as they have been recounted to her. "Even though I wasn't there, I know those moments, their light and their sweetness: that of the park in the autumn when the late dampness climbs from the valley of the Dropt, when all teeming life, fed on the sun, deserts the park and leaves it silent and calm like a church choir after the final service." The parallel with the death of the father continues: "The large park also slept and its silence entered into the room like an enchantment." The interior and the exterior blend together. The young narrator specifies that her mother wanted to have her husband buried in the park, but the property had been sold. And so instead, the young girl goes back to pick a bouquet of roses and place them on his grave. The park, under its different names (Platoriet in this text, Uberan in *Les Impudents,* Les Bugues in *La Vie tranquille*) signifies the father's grave and the daughter's entrance into a literary life.

Duras saw her first two books as "a diversion before attacking" *Un barrage contre le Pacifique.* A detour through the land of her father, in a certain sense, before developing the great myth of the mother. That very French landscape would reemerge, barely changed, more modest but magnified by the discourse and the works that would be born in it, in Marguerite Duras's life itself: in "the house of writing" of Neauphle-le-Château.

In her inimitable voice Duras intones: "I could talk about that house, the garden, for hours. I know everything, I know where the old gates are, everything, the walls of the pond, all the plants, the placement of all the plants, even the wild plants, I know their place, everything." Elsewhere, she lists them: "There, there are thousand-year-old trees and trees that are still young. And there are larches, apple trees, a walnut tree, plum trees, a cherry tree. The apricot tree is dead. In front of my bedroom there is that fabulous rosebush of *L'Homme at-lantique.* A willow. There are also Japanese cherry trees, irises. And under the windows of the music room, there is a camellia, planted for me by Dionys Mascolo" (*Écrire*). This description is a condensed example of the Duras style: repetition, amplification, hyperbole, a mixture of simplicity and preciosity.

Michelle Porte's documentary, *Les Lieux de Marguerite Duras,* the text of which was published in 1977 by Éditions de Minuit, was filmed in Neauphle-le-Château in the house bought in 1958 with the royalties earned from the film based on *Un Bar-rage contre le Pacifique.* Duras bought the house right after she had seen just the park, for a few seconds, and paid on the spot, in cash: "What matters in this Neauphle-le-Château house are the windows onto the park and the road to Paris in front of the house" (*Écrire*). This large garden is also reminiscent of the Le Platier garden. Dionys Mascolo, her companion, redesigned it and planted rosebushes, as he told Duras's biographer, Jean Vallier. Pine trees, purple ashes from America, as well as fruit trees were added to the original larches. There were water lilies on the marshy water that bordered the property.

The garden is visible from the windows; the long shots in Michelle Porte's film show it in the winter or at the very beginning of spring. The terrace is empty, the table and chairs have been put away, the bench is deserted. It's "the first time I have a house to myself," Marguerite Duras points out. From the window, she contemplates the roses while writing. She turned the house and its park into a place of women, for women, those in her novels and films, others too. She explains: when Isabelle Granger walks in the park, she does so as only a woman can do, walking slowly, simply. If a man were to do it, one would think he was reflecting. Writing assumes the restricted space of the bedroom, or of another room in the house, the parlor for example. One can write about the park, in reference to the park, but not in the park. "In the park there are birds, cats. But also once a squirrel, and a ferret. One is not alone in the park" (*Écrire*). The park is too busy, vibrant, rich in multiple lives, to be a place for writing, but it can be a support for it. "I wrote a page recently, I wrote of the humidity of the park, the park dripping with moisture, etc. Then I reread that text, and I saw that I had used plurals. I had written: the humidities of the park. Whereas I had thought of the humidity of the park. [. . .] But it was so much more accurate, in the abundance in the park, the species in the park, to speak of humidities, there was the humidity of the ground, the humidity of the trees, the fruit, the water, the air, etc., it was a plural word . . ." Like Baudelaire, she turned the plural into a singular and a singular into a plural. This life outside, in nature, of the garden, of the pond, is inseparable from the process of writing, from creation, from what brings life to life. Whether in her books or her films, the characters constantly go from the interior to the exterior, like Marguerite Duras's gaze. "It was from looking at the garden through the window, there, through the door, there, that I created Isabelle Granger." She also contemplated the garden from her sickbed placed under a long window in the attic. "My books come out of this house. Out of this light, out of the park. Out of that light reflected on the pond" (*Écrire*).

The garden or the park are also catalysts for creation—as were the sea and the beach in Trouville, where she stayed in the last years of her life; it was as if, after a certain time, Marguerite Duras had abolished all the barriers in herself, and around her. In contrast, gardens delimit a closed, protective perimeter, a prolongation of the house. They encourage reverie, but above all memories. "It's very rare that I walk in my garden in the country, or here, on the beach, without reliving things that are very, that is, immeasurably, distant. It happens in little bursts. And I tell myself that these are the places that contain those memories . . ."

For Marguerite Duras a park is like a crystal ball or coffee grounds for a seer. It enables thought to reconnect with that "state of extremely intense listening to the exterior world," that "deconcentration" that alone encourages writing. The park, a threshold to the forest, is a place of enchantment. It leads to the realm of witches, those medieval women relegated to solitude who, according to Duras, a passionate reader of Michelet, reinvented "intelligence with nature." But above all, it reconnects one to oneself, to that memory of the depths out of which emerge people and words.

The enclosed space of the house, the park, and the adjacent forest is found in almost all of Duras's films: *Détruire dit-elle, India Song, Nathalie Granger, Jaune le soleil.* What does it matter if, in real life, the park of Neauphle-le-Château, if we believe those who were there, was a garden, the music room a simple room with a piano, the pond a marsh, and the house located next to the road! What does it matter if the water tank was outside the bedroom window! What does it matter if it's a war memorial! Only the words that she places on mythologized reality matter: "In the enclosed garden of *L'Homme atlantique,*

177

his despair of his love was in the now abandoned garden. I can still see myself there, alone with my thoughts, caught in the ice of deserted gardens." The "happy misfortune," "the only possible impossible love" transfigure the place into a setting. Always, the "literary park" . . .

. . . Such as that other park, in *Le Ravissement de Lol V. Stein,* impeccable, following strict order, that of the normal life to which Lola Valérie attempts to devote herself following her marriage; for ten years a faithful wife, the mother of three little girls, she confines her madness in the yoke of meticulous rules that reflect the void that surrounds her. Lacking a sense of self and of attachment to her own life, Lol's house and garden can only be modeled upon those of others. In her new S. Tahla house, Lol also takes care of the abandoned garden, but the paths that she has created, which fan out on either side of the porch, don't cross. That design "error" is the first failure in an exhaustingly perfectionist and protective system. The park with impractical paths reveals the mental prison which she will gradually escape only to slip into madness.

Lol's park is the exact opposite of that of her friend Tatiana Karl, whose embraces with her lover resuscitate in Lol, in the form of an obsession, her feelings of being excluded when she witnessed her fiancé, Michaël Richardson, and Anne-Marie Stretter come together as a couple for the first time. For Lol, there is the symmetry of the paths that do not meet up and the protective shrubs that she plans to plant around her house; for Tatiana, there are flower beds, hydrangeas that "fade in the shade of the trees," "their purple flowing," "hydrangeas,

hydrangeas," a landscape over which passes movement, the winds of time and of light—life. Gardens are revealing, projections of our self in space.

The final image in the novel, unforgettable, is that of Lol having fallen asleep in the rye field where she has been watching the romantic encounter of Tatiana and Jacques Hold.

But the Duras book in which gardens occupy a truly significant place is *Le Vice-Consul.* In a reinvented Calcutta, where the topography takes sovereign liberty with reality, a Calcutta that is truer than nature, gardens are everywhere. They form a certain spatial and sensorial leitmotif, they are places in which the characters meet, avoid each other, watch each other, are lost, meet up, flee each other, touch each other. Like a painter who places touches of color on a canvas, Marguerite Duras with a few words reconstructs a tropical nature, in those vast spaces reserved for whites and their servants. Oleander, with its "cloying," "sugary," "funereal" scent, or which sometimes smells like mud, is everywhere. In the park, "the countless Nepalese palms stand immobile": alliterations, phrases with Racine-inspired accents, join the damp heat that infuses the novel night and day. The cries of the birds ring out, echoing those of the vice-consul. This sensuality which involves all of the senses gradually impregnates the reader's imaginary, and places him in the center of the text—provided he abandons himself to it. The gardens of Calcutta—to which should be added that of the white woman who takes the child from the beggar woman in Vinh Long, so similar to Marguerite's childhood garden, with its banana and mango trees—prolong the space of the house; they are both inside and outside; they represent an intermediary, as if magnetized, space, weighed down with passions that unfold in the house, the bedroom, the ballroom—or somewhere else: the river, the sea. The garden unites the land, the sky, the water, and the fire—that oppressive sun veiled by clouds, that stifling heat which is the very essence of tragic poetry.

Every home is associated with a garden: the former house of the vice-consul in Neuilly-sur-Seine, with its lilacs; the ambassador of France's residence in Calcutta, with its oleanders; that of the vice-consul in Lahore; the gardens of Shalimar with their trees under which the lepers sleep; Anne-Marie Stretter's villa on the island, with its giant eucalyptus. Those gardens play a determining role in the dramatic and fictional economy of the novel. It is in the gardens of the embassy that the vice-consul notices Anne-Marie Stretter for the first time, that he watches her, dreaming a melancholy dream, or follows her to the deserted tennis courts, notices her bicycle leaning against a fence. These gardens where she walks with her daughters, plays tennis, or rides a bicycle illustrate both the daily life of the ambassador's wife and her power of seduction, her powerful charm over men. The topography of the place is as precise as it would be in a dream: there are the buildings of the embassy grounds, the dependencies with the kitchens where Anne-Marie Stretter sees that water is given to the lepers, and in the back, the tennis courts and the paths where she walks. These gardens, enclosed by fences and protected by guards, are also the location of the exercise of colonial power; attachés and guests pass through them, as do gardeners responsible for maintaining them. They render concrete the separation that exists between the colonial world and the world of the lepers and the beggar woman, sitting under the trees on the other side of the boulevard that goes along the Ganges. It is a policed world, an elegant world, subject to boredom and frivolity in the face of a world of poverty and suffering.

In Lahore, in the gardens of Shalimar, the vice-consul's despair is expressed violently in an "impossible" act: people say that one night he shot at the lepers who were lying in the shade of the trees. Those deserted gardens of Shalimar, which inspire the author's incantatory poetry, which are never described, barely evoked, are at the origin of the vice-consul's exile, and perhaps of his solitude, of his banishment from society. They appear strangely different from the "true" gardens of Shalimar in Kashmir, described with admiration by the doctor François Bernier in the seventeenth century, an example of that sublime art of Islamic gardens in India. But of course, Duras the magician knew the fascinating power of names . . .

Like a leitmotif, the air of *India Song* follows the vice-consul through the gardens of the French embassy, gardens that are stifling as they wait for the summer monsoon, nocturnal gardens with sleeping birds, the palm grove of the island where Anne-Marie Stretter and her faithful escorts take refuge to escape from Calcutta; the landscapes of Marguerite Duras are pure literary constructions, which would be reinterpreted in her film *India Song*.

Far from the realism or the picturesque of what an "adaptation" could be—she railed against that of *L'Amant*—Duras chose the Rothschild villa in Boulogne-sur-Seine to portray the

French embassy in Calcutta. Run-down, old-fashioned, surrounded by a badly maintained park, it creates the setting for the film, giving an unrivaled depth and melancholy to the wanderings of Delphine Seyrig and her admirers, accompanied by the enchanting music of Carlos d'Alessio. The reader/viewer is free to imagine the gardens of Shalimar or Calcutta . . . or to remember that "literary park," so distant, so far, in the land of Duras.

THE INVISIBLE GARDENS OF
PATRICK MODIANO

In search of lost ivy . . .

His huge frame, his beauty, his increasingly abstracted gaze, his muted and hesitant voice, that "something" that is childlike, dreamy, and stubborn make Patrick Modiano the most attractive ghost of our contemporary literature. Wandering in his company; traveling through the transparency of his language; encountering familiar places as we turn the pages of his books, while not really knowing where we encountered them before; meeting characters who are not completely familiar, yet not completely unknown—to experience the delight of that flickering of one's memory makes reading his novels a disconcerting experience. His Paris is mine, his characters resemble those that wander in my dreams. In his Paris I even find the places where I've lived, like those perimeter boulevards or, in *Pour que tu ne te perdes pas dans le quartier,* Square Graisivaudan, where I was born. Obsessive, repetitive, piercing, vertiginous, like a flurry of snow, a monotonous falling of rain on the pavement—the uninterrupted monologue of a solitary being who drifts away . . . I discovered all this with the publication of *La Place de l'Étoile,* Modiano's first book. Was I too young? I had a sense of both familiarity and foreignness. That Place de l'Étoile, where I used to go when I was a teenager, was not the one I knew. In my personal mythology, the Occupation evoked memories of my mother, seeking refuge in the Poitou, swimming in the Vienne, her triumphant twenties. Modiano's underworld, the issue of his paternal mythology, was unrecognizable to me, the puzzle pieces didn't fit.

However, with *Villa triste,* so "New Wave," so "Italian film from the 1960s," with its lakeside town, its palaces, its sleepwalking hero seeking his lost loves, I engaged in a staccato dialogue with Modiano's work, a waffling whose intensity I later understood when I read *Dora Bruder.* That Dora was like the sister of another Dora whose story I had myself written a few years earlier. In my story, a man pursues a woman he has just seen in a café; it doesn't involve the Occupation or Jews, rather a mysterious disappearance, a pursuit, and a murder in the same place as in Modiano's novel: boulevard Rochechouart.

So, what a strange idea to look for gardens in his work! Modiano, the most urban of novelists, whose books, page after page, list the names of streets, travel the city, describing an urban landscape that is both inorganic and uncertain; Modiano, the pedestrian of Paris—and sometimes of provincial cities that he passes through like distant suburbs of the capital . . . Would I have even thought of him if not for Anny DR, who one day reminded me of a garden in *Rue des boutiques obscures?*

Everything occurs as if nature were invisible, or absent from his books. Eyes raised up to the names of streets, to dark windows and lighted signs, or noses lowered to the ground—the reader is drawn in by the topographical poetry of a city whose proper names suggest a geography that seems less real, despite appearances, more cerebral, sensate, or sometimes even dreamlike.

Gardens? Yes.

We might give these barely seen gardens the title of one of Modiano's novels: *L'Herbe des nuits.* Far from serving as simple descriptive fillers, they are endowed with profound meaning, impregnated with the scent of the past and, at the same time, resolutely modern. Those wastelands, those "gardens full of shadow," those bits of nature growing between paving stones or along a park, evoke "neutral zones" in which Roland, one of the protagonists of *Dans le café de la jeunesse perdue,* is interested: "In Paris there were intermediary zones, 'no man's lands' where you were on the edge of everything, in transit, or even in limbo. We enjoyed a certain immunity there." Of course, for Roland, those places were above all streets, passages, deserted sidewalks. But to the square Cambronne, to the neighborhood between Ségur and Dupleix, to the rue d'Argentine, and to other "neutral zones," we might add, metaphorically, gardens. Isn't the completely relative immunity that one can enjoy in these neutral spaces just another way of "going into the green," as expressed by the father of the narrator in *Un pedigree,* of fleeing danger, being sheltered? Roland chose a pseudonym to avoid attracting attention to himself and because "[his] true name was too exotic." As for Patoche, the narrator in *Remise de peine* who escapes from middle school, he goes to Chantilly, Mortefontaine, Ermenonville, and the abbey of Chaalis, whose parks are at the heart of Nerval's poetic geography.

In *Dora Bruder,* Patrick Modiano himself notes the troubling coincidence between the true story of a young Jewish girl who in 1941 went missing from the boarding school of Saint-Coeur-de-Marie at 62, rue de Picpus and that of Cosette and Jean Valjean, who seek refuge at the same address, in the convent garden: "a sort of very vast, quite unusual-looking garden; one of those sad gardens that seem meant to be seen in winter and at night . . . grass had invaded half of it and green moss covered the rest." If Dora Bruder, like Cosette, had, instead of fleeing, chosen "not to leave, to remain forgotten, in the shadow of these black walls," she would have perhaps escaped arrest and deportation. "Yes, the only hideaway that still existed was the garden and the courtyard of the school of Saint-Coeur-de-Marie." To have remained there, Dora, like Cosette, needed to have been directed by the sure hand of a utopian novelist.

Gardens constitute many "intermediary" zones, both in the city and outside it; zones that are sometimes made wild, like the uncultivated lands that are celebrated by certain landscape artists today. The celebration of wanderers and wandering, the Modiano garden is halfway between real landscapes and memory, walked along, passed through, relived, bringing with it the gusts of scents or dreams, adjusting the geometry of streets and buildings. It is one with the flow of the evocation, its foliage masking the rigidity of a wall, the nakedness of a façade, the permanence of a memory.

But nature—a blade of grass, the petal of a flower, a tree—can also provide comfort in moments of despair or of a passage into emptiness, like the *charme* (hornbeam tree) or the *tremble* (aspen) (two words chosen of course for their polysemy) at Daragane's window in *Pour que tu ne te perdes pas dans le quartier.*

These gardens in the city are primarily public parks which characters encounter during their quests or their wanderings: the Jardin des Plantes, the Parc Monceau, the Luxembourg, the Jardins du Louvre, those of the Palais-Royal, the Parc Montsouris, the Jardins des Champs-Élysées or, more often, the Jardins des Tuileries. In *Rue des boutiques obscures,* Guy Roland (he, too, adopted that first name as a pseudonym) and his girlfriend Denise go through a Paris at night, "summery and unreal," where the red and green lights marked a time that was as regular and soft as the swaying of palms. "We were floating in a night perfumed by the privet shrubs by the fence when we passed in front of the Parc Monceau." We find those privets again in other Modiano novels; with plane trees, they constitute the essential urban vegetation and surround gardens like a protective barrier. Privet hedges, plane trees: nothing could be more commonplace.

In contrast, Nice or Annecy stand out owing to the exotic touches provided by the palm trees, the eucalyptus, the mimosas, or even the birch tree with a silvery trunk in the garden of the Russian church in Nice, sketching a composite landscape. In *Villa triste,* the English gardens of the former palaces of Annecy serve as settings for the vain quest for lost paradise. Victor Chmara (another pseudonym) returns to Annecy, on the trail of a love from his youth: "In the summer, the gardens of the Hermitage, the Windsor, and the Alhambra closely resembled one's image of those of Eden or the Promised Land." A path under a bower of purple and blue clematis, laburnum, "rock-dwelling plants of frosted hues," pink hawthorns and beds of yellow, red, and white dahlias turn the park into an idyllic setting for Victor and Yvonne's romantic encounter. The brilliant colors, to which are added the young woman's red hair and her green dress, reflect the radiance that is associated with happy times. Returning to the place some dozen years later, Victor sadly notes that of those splendors "there remained only a few dead and rotting trees." Is it his memory that has deformed the past, or has that radiant place of happiness been transformed into a dying little provincial town?

The Jardins des Tuileries are the domain par excellence of childhood. In *Villa triste,* Victor recognizes the strange person who once sailed a miniature replica of the *Kon-Tiki* on the water of the garden basins. In *Un pedigree,* the most autobiographical of Patrick Modiano's novels, the Tuileries are described at length: "On the other side of the Seine, mysteries of the courtyard of the Louvre, the two squares of the Carrousel and the Jardins des Tuileries where I spent long afternoons with my brother. Black stone and the leaves of the chestnut trees in the sun. The theater of green. The mountain of dead leaves against the wall beneath the terrace, below the Jeu de Paume museum. [. . .] The gardeners. The whirring sound of the lawnmower, one sunny morning, on the grass, near the basin." That luminous autumn is inscribed forever in the author's memory, with "the clock whose immobile hands have stopped for all eternity," and "the red scar branded on Milady's shoulder." Suspended time, a disgraceful branding: signs that are incorporated in the personal mythology of the author of

La Place de l'Étoile. The two children create genealogical *trees* of the kings of France. "Our challenge was to find the connection between Saint Louis and Henri IV." The essence of the Modiano identity quest is encapsulated in the two brothers' game: how can one bring together events of the past, avoid gaps, uncertainties, errors, find the connection between shattered, fragmented facts. Patrick would soon create those genealogical "trees" alone. His little brother, Rudy, died of leukemia at the age of ten. The Tuileries retained the image of those sunny days the two brothers spent together. That lost paradise could only be found again in dreams, or perhaps in writing.

An almost surreal light haloes the evocations of gardens associated with childhood, between memory and conscious dream. In *Rue des boutiques obscures* Guy Roland and Denise take a little girl to the park of Versailles. They walk along the paths and row a boat. The sun reflects brilliantly on the water. The ice cream the little girl eats is green and pink. This colorized escape seems like a photo that is blurred because of being overexposed. In addition, Roland doesn't know who this little girl is, and that isolated memory will assume its place in the course of events only later in the novel. That mystery, that vagueness, constitute the very essence of memory, but also the mark of an ill-defined identity. "The more things remained obscure and mysterious," notes the Modiano of *Un pedigree,* "the more I was interested in them." That quest for meaning is rooted in childhood and, like a rhizome, feeds the entire structure of the novel.

And so the childhood memory can sometimes be warped by what is learned later in life. Like the happy memories of the Bois de Boulogne, with the scent of its leaves penetrating the calm streets of Auteuil, that metamorphose into nauseating suspicion. On Sunday, Patoche and his brother take the no. 63 bus with their father to the Bois de Boulogne. Elements of the landscape describe the setting of a privileged childhood: "The lake and the pier where you set off to play miniature golf and for the Chalet des Îles . . ." But one evening, on the way home, they stop in front of a house on the rue Adolphe-Yvon, which later causes the memory to be altered. The now adult narrator learns that at that address during the Occupation was the "Otto Bureau," the black market headquarters in Paris: "And suddenly a stench of rot blended with the smell of the stables and the dead leaves in the Bois" (*Un pedigree*). Rot retrospectively destroys the very fabric of memory.

Similarly, in *Rue des boutiques obscures,* the serenity of Guy Roland and Denise's strolls around Monceau deteriorates when the evocation is associated with the memory of sketchy dealings concerning jewelry: "The weather had changed. The snow was falling and I could scarcely recognize the street, with its naked trees, the black façades of its buildings. No more smell of privets along the fence of the Parc Monceau, only an odor of damp earth and rot." The Parc Monceau and the Bois de Boulogne—in those western neighborhoods so integral to Modiano's fictional geography (and to that of Marcel Proust)—are the first places affected by the rotting of relived sensations which always accompanies any mention of the Occupation, the piercing echo of the mysterious activities of Albert Modiano, the author's father, during that period. "Rot"—mightn't that be the insult inscribed in the deterioration of the paternal image? Like the humus of gardens, memory in Modiano is made up of scattered recollections, repetitive, fragmentary, cut off from their roots, decomposed. But that decomposition also feeds the fertile earth of the work.

Like memory, the city is scattered with hideouts, "gardens full of shadow" surrounded by walls where, in the fading light of dusk, a few restaurant tables bathe in an atmosphere of mystery and melancholia. Near the Faubourg Saint-Honoré, the Castille Hotel, where Guy Roland, a former private detective who has lost his memory, goes in search of his own past, opens onto "a courtyard with walls hung with green trellises covered in ivy." In *Dans le café de la jeunesse perdue,* Roland also looks for any trace of a building where a certain Guy de Vere once lived. More exactly, he wants to know if there really had been ivy on the front of that building.

"You are incorrigible, Roland, with your story of ivy. I knew you when you were very young, right? How old were you?"

"Twenty years old."

"Well, it seems to me that even at that age, you were already off in search of lost ivy."

That "search for lost ivy," besides the fact that it pleasantly reveals a connection between Marcel Proust and Patrick Modiano, symbolizes the details that are attached to the deceptive façade of our certainties and enable us to renew the bond between past and present. Like the madeleine or the paving stones in Venice for Proust, ivy can be a catalyst. But in Modiano, time can never be rediscovered, because every clue relates only to a fragmented, vanished, or inaccessible reality. To retrace one's steps is to encounter deterioration or nothingness.

The novel becomes a deceptive quest for a vanished world, or one that perhaps never really existed except in the narrator's imagination.

Like intermediate zones between the past and the present, abandoned gardens thus emerge, lawns with overgrown grass. Remember the wonderful garden on the rue Plumet in *Les Misérables,* where "gardening had departed, and nature had returned. The weeds were abundant, an admirable adventure for a poor bit of land." But what is splendor and the strength of the vital force in Hugo, which turns the "nasty little Parisian garden" into a virgin forest in the New World, takes on a completely different meaning in Modiano.

In *Rue des boutiques obscures,* an initial tableau prefigures the key scene in the novel: "One of the façades of the building faced a square that appeared abandoned. A large group of trees, shrubs, some grass that hadn't been weeded for a long time. A child played all alone, peacefully, in front of a pile of sand that sunny late afternoon." The image of that abandoned square, across from the Auteuil racetrack, appears again a few pages later in Valbreuse, where Guy Roland goes in search of his own childhood and identity. "The grass grew up to my knees and I tried to cross the lawn as quickly as possible, going toward the chateau. That silent building intrigued me. I feared discovering that behind the façade there would only be more tall grass and expanses of crumbling walls." A metaphor for that uncultivated memory, the abandoned garden, with its so Nervalian "long brick and stone building, in the Louis XIII style," also evokes the Montcel school in Jouy-en-Josas, where as a child Patrick Modiano was a boarding student. That ruined chateau also appears in *Remise de peine,* associated with the same image of a "meadow of tall grass" where the children dive in up to their waists. The same abandoned park that then becomes a clearing in *Chien de printemps.*

In *Rue des boutiques obscures,* at the end of a path near the lawn, there is a labyrinth, carefully maintained by a gardener who Guy Roland hopes will be able to confirm his identity. The description equates the labyrinth with a network of urban roads, with "intersections, roundabouts, circular or right-angle turns." Its geometric structure contrasts with the weedy lawn. It alone seems to have escaped the deterioration of time. Will it enable the hero, armed with that Ariadne's thread—the intact memory of the gardener, guardian of the labyrinth—to discover who he is? "As a child, I must have played hide-and-seek here with my grandfather or with friends my age, in the middle of that magical maze that smells like privets and pines." Just like the rusty frame from which two swings were hung, it awakens in Guy Roland a nostalgia for a normal, carefree childhood, with a family and playmates. As with each possibly happy evocation, a "tender and orange-infused" light appears.

But the labyrinth can only reveal the complexity of a quest for identity. Its pathways constitute a lure. The gardener doesn't recognize him as Freddie Howard de Luz, the little boy who lived in the chateau. "I had never played in the 'labyrinth' as a child. The swings on that rusty frame had not been hung for me. Pity." Modiano, like his character, is a resigned Theseus who wanders endlessly in the labyrinth of his memory. "I was nothing, but waves went through me, sometimes distant, sometimes stronger, and all those scattered echoes that floated in the air crystallized, and that was me" (*Rue des boutiques obscures*). "Weeds" cover the green childhood paradises, and neither gardens nor labyrinths can deliver the definitive key to an existence whose foundations have definitively crumbled. "Snippets, bits of something, suddenly came back to me during my search . . . But in the end, perhaps that is what a life is . . . ," concludes the hero of the novel before, in a final effort, he considers going back to his old address, "on the street of obscure shops," the *via delle Botteghe Oscure,* on the edge of the former Jewish ghetto in Rome, that other, oh, how meaningful, labyrinth where his identity was lost.

Unless, like the narrator of *Chien de printemps,* the novelist himself disappears one day in the crowd of the Jardin du Luxembourg, a familiar place for strolling, after having made every effort to "exercise a profession, give coherence to [his] life, attempt to speak and write a language as well as possible," and, like the hero in *Pour que tu ne te perdes pas dans le quartier,* finally to be a "Buffon of trees and flowers."

Like a Tree in the City

Although urban ecology is not all that recent—it comes
from the Chicago school at the beginning of the twentieth
century—global warming makes a reduction of greenhouse
gas emissions in cities quite urgent. Successive "climate
plans" have developed different ways for us to confront
this challenge in Paris. Urban "greening," or the creation of
all forms of green spaces, is part of this. Hundreds of parks,
gardens, and squares already exist in Paris, most the result
of the work of Haussmann and Adolphe Alphand. More
recent ones have appeared, inspired by an ecological conception of diversity, such as the Parc André-Citroën, the
Parc Georges-Brassens, the Jardin Serge-Gainsbourg above
the highway at the Porte des Lilas, and the natural garden
of wild plants on the rue de la Réunion.

The southern Coulée verte, from Châtillon to Massy; the
Petite Ceinture between Auteuil and La Muette; the Jardins
d'Éole; or the Coulée verte René-Dumont between Bastille and Reuilly, built on the sites of abandoned railroad
tracks, introduce nature into the urban landscape. Num-
bers of shared gardens, heirs of family gardens, are appearing in vacant lots or between buildings, enabling those living there not only to grow food but also to forge social
relationships. There is an increase in green walls or roofs;
hanging gardens, like the 8,000 square meters of grasses

above the shopping center of Beaugrenelle in the fifteenth *arrondissement;* inner courtyards being transformed into gardens. Finally, the "green" and "blue" corridors, defined by French law and found for example in Nantes, named European Green Capital in 2013, aim to preserve ecological continuity in the urban and peri-urban fabric. The landscapes of cities and suburbs are opening to nature. It's a matter of survival.

CHRISTIAN BOBIN,
GARDENER IN PARADISE

Life would be nothing without contemplation.

"The TGV station is in the middle of nowhere, but you'll see, it's pretty, there's grass." I didn't see it: the SNCF was on strike and we had reached Le Creusot in our car, in spite of the gusty wind and the rain mixed with snow. Nothing would have prevented me from going. The prize was at the end of the path: warm tea and cookies to welcome us and, above all, the childlike smile and blue eyes of Christian Bobin, his warm simplicity. It was the most beautiful encounter in fifteen years of writing articles on the homes of writers. Walking with him in the grey streets of Le Creusot, contemplating a dead leaf on the ground, the worn trunk of a plane tree, the house where he—and his father—were born, shivering in the dampness while he strolled along with his shirt collar open wearing only a corduroy jacket, coming in to the warmth of the little apartment in a former firehouse: one listens to Christian Bobin the way one reads his books—between the mysterious and the self-evident. There are flowers everywhere: marigolds, anemones, tulips, and on the windowsill a sun-yellow chrysanthemum. We left, the photographer Gilbert Nencioli and I, under the hold of a spell, that of a man who is alive, present, and free.

Gardens are everywhere and nowhere in Christian Bobin's books. In a certain way, they *are* his books. Flowers bloom and fade under his attentive gaze: blue hydrangeas in the narrow courtyard of his childhood, glittering roses in vases, or brightly colored tulips, as in the drawings of children, irises, daisies, violets, primroses, morning glories along the wall, Christ-blue periwinkles, daisies, buttercups and dandelions, the most humble of creatures, the most joyful for the eye of the poet. Like a flower its petals, Bobin has disseminated some fifty books. His roots plunge into the black dirt of despair. However, out of solitude and silence there burst forth radiant words.

For Bobin, the garden is associated with games of childhood innocence, such as the make-believe tea of a child's tea party on the grass (*L'Inespérée*). "The birds in the garden were unaware of the existence of evil," notes the author of *Le Très-Bas,* a book dedicated to Francis Assisi. The memory of a tomato stolen from a neighbor's garden is a "burst of heroic childhood," a gift to him from the little boy, the story told to a five-and-a-half-year-old girl whose mother has just died. "Joy is round like a tomato. It is a red sun given by the neighbor [. . .]. So, frog, in every instance and in every second of your life: bon appétit" (*Autoportrait au radiateur*). The beloved woman, suddenly gone, is compared to "a child whom a distant song attracts in the garden." Perhaps she returned to that vast field that she loved as a little girl? Even the flowers have something childlike about them. The flowers of the old cherry tree chatter. Nine tulips in a vase "puff with laughter," and Christian Bobin declares: "I love you, girls." After the death of G., he buys two bouquets of flowers every week, a way of "feeding the invisible ones" that surround him. He talks to them, they keep him company in his solitude. His gaze lingers on their blossoming and their decline. Flowers teach us about the ephemeral: "What makes things happen is that which is living, and that which is living cannot keep itself from being lost." Or, in *La Grande Vie:* "The blossoming of the cherry trees doesn't last. We grasp the essential in a second. The rest is useless." To describe paintings with flowers, rather than the French expression *nature morte,* we should use the English "still life": a tranquil life. For Bobin, it's a question of opposing closing up and depression with the beauty of the world, as is sung in a beautiful passage in *Autoportrait au radiateur.* The poet "has a meeting every morning with the beauty of the world." It is found in everything in our daily lives; we need only know how to look at it.

For example, it is found in abandoned gardens where weeds run wild, in the sun of a dandelion, or the cheerful modesty of a daisy. It is also found in a simple crack in a wall where a tuft of grass has found a home, or in the abandoned garden which "buttercups set on fire" (*Une bibliothèque de nuages*). The poet's preference is for those uncultivated gardens, such as that "wide band of grassy land, illuminated by dreaming fruit trees," which hides its poverty behind a fence on a street in Le Creusot, the town where he has lived for a long time, now a stone's throw from the place where he was born. They provide neither flowers, nor fruits, nor vegetables. These urban spaces, between two buildings, deliver themselves up to nature alone, and that is what creates the beauty of their tall grass. It is less their wild state that attracts the one who sees them than their solitude and the all-powerfulness of life. They also symbolize the redemption of the disinherited. "God adopts abandoned gardens, placing a hand of cool wind on their feverish grass. There is nothing forgotten by the world that isn't known and exalted by the unseen" (*Une bibliothèque de nuages*).

As in Patrick Modiano, abandoned gardens offer the "beautiful madness of childhood," its hope and its joy, in contrast to overly maintained lawns, mowed grass, well-organized beds of disciplined flowers. The short grass of "green melancholia" imposes its rigidity, without life and death, thanks to the care of a gardener without imagination: "What devotion, what rectitude in boredom, what loyalty in lassitude." The impeccable lawns of the center for the mentally handicapped in Le Creusot also remind him of the little green spaces of the "houses of owners," large bourgeois homes or more modest villas. The "tamed" green of their grass is not the result of a mix of blue and yellow, but of the grey and black of monotony and possession. The lawns bear witness to a strict order, that which encloses the mad and encloses the houses of the rich.

A peaceful anarchy hides behind Bobin's apparently naive optimism. There is something antisocial in him. The winds of freedom that blow over his words make gypsies his brothers. His gardens are less imaginary than growing from his heart. Like that of Emily Dickinson, his chosen sister, whose world stopped at her garden, "her church," then at her house, then at her bedroom, which she would never leave.

But gardens also appear as metaphors for the work of the writer or for the field which is his. The linden tree at his window inspires masterful writing. How is it possible to write with so much grace: "that tree, delicately inscribing its light and shadow on each of its leaves, and renewing its inspiration every second" (*Ressusciter*)? The images seen in between are "like a garden one senses behind a door, or like a jolt of light glimpsed through a bower" (*Autoportrait au radiateur*). Bobin speaks of little things, the infinitesimal real that alone protects from disaster. "I do what is very small, I bear witness for a blade of grass." We mustn't see that as false modesty, rather as a strong will to resist the disorder and the decay of the world. Bobin doesn't dream of a pacified world; he wages a battle for the joy that is often hidden in the tiny things of everyday life. This "blade of grass theory" is one of the elements of the "inexhaustible": the beauty of the world is within our reach provided we know how to see it, the chestnut shell that has fallen on the ground, a mismatched porcelain cup, a snowflake, or that linden tree at the window which announces the seasons.

This is perhaps what makes Christian Bobin's most beautiful books, to me, the simplest of them all, those least invaded by metaphors, the most compelling; books by a Bobin who mischievously reproaches the phrase in Proust that is believed to be "more beautiful than the hawthorn it describes" (*La Lumière du monde*). Yes, how does one speak of "life's refusal to speechify"?

It's not enough simply to see. "The tyranny of the visible makes us all blind" (*La Dame blanche*). The garden, like the meadow, is also a mirror of the soul and of the infinite. Life is compared to a ramshackle tool shed in the back of a garden. That is where God resides. Bobin's God is not the one of pomp, of rituals, and of churches. He "arrives stumbling from the back of the garden in his moth-eaten clothes" (*La Grande Vie*). He is born of the contemplation and the celebration of the living, however fragile it might be, but also from the awareness of the invisible. This presupposes a distancing with the world, the "root of sweetness" (Emily Dickinson), in the image, perhaps, of the "*Noli me tangere*" of the Christ/gardener, the Jesus resuscitated on Easter Day whom Mary Magdalene takes for a gardener. "Books are paper cloisters. One can walk in them day and night. The garden at the center of the cloisters symbolizes paradise. With time I have become a gardener in paradise, each morning passing an ink rake over a narrow land of white paper. Everything must be harmonious: paradise isn't made for us to live in, but for us to contemplate, and, with a single glance at it, for the soul to be comforted" (*Les Ruines du ciel*).

That is perhaps the ultimate lesson of the garden—if a lesson there is. It is there to comfort. To bear witness to the light for the living. "To live: to walk along a wall until you find a luminous breach. I have found such fissures in the blinding yellow of dandelions, those poor relatives of the sun. I proceed very slowly. I will die without ever reaching the back of the garden" (*Une bibliothèque de nuages*). Each book of *L'Homme-Joie* adds a little more white gravel on our own path. The mystics, the sages, and the poets help us to travel on it by capturing a bit of the meaning of that which escapes us. Christian Bobin is one of them: "I am alive, seated at a wooden table, I am looking at the light shining down on the garden—what more could I ask for?" (*Les Ruines du ciel*).

"MOVING GARDENS"

There are no gardens, there is the Earth.

—Gilles Clément

Indian summer has thrown gold into the garden. It's not as dry as it usually is during this season, since August was rainy; it provides us, along with the purple asters and the yellow cone-flowers, a green lawn and armfuls of roses and late raspberries. Not everything is glorious, far from it. A few rose bushes, struck down by the humidity, hold out their bare branches. Our attempts at a flower-filled set-aside have yielded nothing, except for some spotty grass and a few cottony shoots. Next winter we will have to prune the plum tree and the old cherry tree that is already losing its leaves. In this residential suburb everyone tends his garden with care. I can see the impeccable hedges and the hydrangeas of one, I glimpse the rhododendrons of another, I take advantage of the chestnut, the plum, and the pine trees of a third, the acacias along the train tracks, the maple trees on the roundabout. On the other side of the tracks, in the Marly forest, the first chestnut shells have fallen from the trees. A garden is always inscribed in an environment, whether in a natural setting or in a peri-urban zone like here. The wind, the birds, the insects, the dogs and cats, our own feet, even the wheels of cars, transport seeds and create surprises. Here, on the edge of the street, a tulip. How did it get there? In front of the veranda, between two rose bushes, there's a giant plant that resembles a tree mallow. Who planted that monster? A garden always oscillates between wildness and cultivation. In Normandy, the power of nature is such that I sometimes despair of imposing any order onto the mess. Brambles, dandelions, nettles, you can tell me they are "weeds," that they play their role in the great ecological picture; I fear their invasion, I see them as enemies. Yes, I know, there is fertilizer or nettle soup, dandelion salad, the bright yellow of their flowers . . . But they put my need for dominance to the test. I didn't invite those interlopers. I struggle, in spite of my efforts, to appreciate their beauty.

A garden, explains Gilles Clément, is an enclosure intended to cultivate the best—the best fruit, the best flowers. We protect life in them. Extending the notion of garden to the entire planet enables us to understand just how greatly diversity— and consequently life itself—is threatened today. Observe what is growing, encourage plants that are happy, don't force-feed with fertilizer those that aren't acclimated, intervene as little as possible—those are the rules of the "moving garden" according to Clément. We pay benevolent attention. A bit like with adolescents, actually. I try my hand at that "wisdom of the gardener." But I don't forget that every conception of the garden is first of all cultural, and that that conception, like all others, will perhaps pass . . .

"To anyone who wants to really look," writes Gilles Clément, "everything is art. Nature, the city, the landscape, what is
current, what we call humor, and, ultimately ruling over everything, light" (*Traité succinct de l'art involontaire*).

This is why I include the gardens of novels among the
ephemeral gardens that have decorated the planet for thousands of years. I took my first steps under their paper shading.
Are they less elusive? Hardly. One day they will disappear in
turn, we will no longer understand them. Who still reads, for
pleasure, *La Nouvelle Héloïse* or *Le Lys dans la vallée*? Already, in
contemporary French novels we encounter fewer gardens, it
seems. Perhaps they have scattered and we must go elsewhere
to find them?

And yet, gardens have never evoked such enthusiasm from
the public. Pleasure gardens, royal vegetable gardens, urban
gardens, shared, family gardens, gardens of inclusion, plant
festivals; there is a fever of consumerism seen in Sunday gardeners, garden centers . . . Gardens are both the products of
and the antidote to our civilization. The gardens of writers are
not to be outdone. In Vulaines, in Seine-et-Marne, the landscape gardener Florence Dreyfus reconstructed the garden
of Stéphane Mallarmé with the help of the many details in
his correspondence. At Colette's house, in Saint-Sauveur-en-
Puisaye, they are re-creating—a miracle!—Sido's garden. I can
already smell its scents. In Malagar, the bowers still lead to
the stone bench on the terrace where François Mauriac looked
out over the landscape. The great oak tree that as a child he
hugged when he left Saint-Symphorien was destroyed during

the storms of 1999. I had kept a piece of its bark which had fallen on the ground, but it burned in the fire in my house, last year. After the wind, and the water, the fire.

In the time it has taken to reread these pages, November is now coming to an end. Night is falling earlier and earlier. Leaves cover the lawn. We have pruned the rose bushes. The purple of the hydrangeas is turning brown, the heather is flowering. Other trees, other flowers will come. The great agitation of time spares neither writing nor nature. But it is our duty in spite of everything to watch over and protect the treasures that have been bequeathed to us. Novels we have loved, gardens we have dreamed of, gardens of the future, gardens of the planet: "We must now look after the living. Consider it. Know it. Become its friend," as Gilles Clément also said. Perhaps this is what is called "passing down."

ACKNOWLEDGMENTS

I want to thank my dear Manuel Carcassonne, who has accompanied me in my work for so very many years—and, I hope, for many more years to come.

My thanks to the entire team at Stock, and particularly to Capucine Ruat, whose pretty first name enables me to add a final flower to these paper gardens.

Some of the material included here was first written for my courses at the Université populaire du gout d'Argentan. It has been greatly reworked and developed.

LITERARY WORKS DISCUSSED IN THE TEXT

"I WENT DOWN TO MY GARDEN . . ."

Virginia Woolf, *The Voyage Out* (1915)

François-René de Chateaubriand, *Mémoires d'outretombe* (1848-50)

Countess de Ségur, *Les Vacances* (1859)

A BIT OF HISTORY

Roman de la Rose (Guillaume de Lorris, c. 1230; Jean de Meun, c. 1275)

Horace, *Satires* (35 BC)

Charlemagne, *Capitulare de Villis* (c. 771-800)

Pietro de Crescenzi, *Ruralia commode,* sometimes known as the *Liber ruralium commodorum* (Book of rural benefits), (c. 1304-9)

Boccacio, *Decameron* (1353)

Leon Battista Alberti, *De re aedificatoria* (1443-52)

Francesco Colonna, *Hypnerotomachia Poliphili* (1499)

Erasmus, "The Religious Banquet" (1526)

Bernard Palissy, *Récepte véritable par laquelle tous les hommes de la France pourront apprendre à multiplier et augmenter leurs trésors* (1563)

Claude Mollet, *Théâtre des plans et jardinages* (1652)

Olivier de Serres, *Le Théâtre d'agriculture et mésnage des champs* (1600)

René Descartes, *Discours de la méthode* (1637)

Salomon de Caus, *La Perspective avec la raison des ombres et des miroirs* (1612)

Jacques Boyceau, *Traité de jardinage selon les raisons de la nature et de l'art* (1638)

René Descartes, *Dioptrique* (1637)

André Mollet, *Le Jardin de plaisir* (1651)

Jean de La Fontaine, *"Le Songe de Vaux—Éloge des jardins"* (1671)

Madeleine de Scudéry, *Clélie* (1654-61)

Louis XIV, *Manière de montrer les jardins de Versailles* (1689-1705)

Jean de La Fontaine, *Les Amours de Psyché et de Cupidon* (1699)

Louis de Rouvroy, duc de Saint-Simon, *Mémoires* (1700)

Alexander Pope, "Epistle IV" (1731)

William Hogarth, *The Analysis of Beauty* (1753)

Christian Cajus Lorenz Hirschfeld, *Theorie der Gartenkunst, 5 vols.* (1779-85)

Thomas Whately, *Observations on Modern Gardening* (1777)

Claude-Henri Watelet, *Essai sur les jardins* (1774)

René-Louis de Girardin, *De la composition des paysages* (1777)

JEAN-JACQUES ROUSSEAU, OR THE INVENTION OF NATURE

Jean-Jacques Rousseau, *Rêveries du promeneur solitaire* (1782)

Bernardin de Saint-Pierre, *La Vie et les ouvrages de Jean-Jacques Rousseau* (1907)

Jean-Jacques Rousseau, *Julie, ou la nouvelle Heloïse* (1761)

Jean-Jacques Rousseau, *Confessions* (1770)

Jean-Jacques Rousseau, *Du contrat sociale* (1762)

Alexander Pope, "Epistle IV" (1731)

Horace Walpole, *On Modern Gardening* (1780)

Jean-Jacques Rousseau, *Émile, ou de l'education* (1762)

Jean-Jacques Rousseau, *Lettres écrites de la montagne* (1764)

Jean-Jacques Rousseau, *Lettres élémentaires sur la botanique* (1782)

Prince de Ligne, *Coup d'oeil sur Beloeil* (1781)

WE MUST CULTIVATE OUR GARDENS

Voltaire, *Candide, ou l'optimisme* (1759)

GEORGE SAND, OR THE NATURAL GARDEN

Henry James, *George Sand* (1878)

George Sand, *Histoire de ma vie* (1855)

Aurore Sand, "Souvenirs de Nohant," *Revue de Paris,* September 1, 1916, 81-109.

George Sand and Alexandre Monceau, *Agendas* (c. 1865)

George Sand, *"Ce que disent les fleurs,"* in *Contes d'une grand-mère* (1873)

George Sand, *Nouvelles Lettres d'un voyageur* (1877)

George Sand, *La Rêverie à Paris* (1876)

George Sand, *Le Pays des anémones* (1877)

George Sand, *Un Hiver à Majorque* (1842)

George Sand *La Daniella* (1857)

George Sand, *Mauprat* (1837)

George Sand, *Le Meunier d'Angibault* (1845)

George Sand, *Le Péché de monsieur Antoine* (1847)

A PASSION FOR FLOWERS

Étienne Pierre Ventenat and Pierre-Joseph Redouté, *Le Jardin de la Malmaison* (1803)

Charlotte de La Tour, *Langage des fleurs* (1819)

LOVE IN THE GARDEN: BALZAC, STENDHAL, FLAUBERT, HUGO, ZOLA

Jacques-Henri Bernardin de Saint-Pierre, *Paul et Virginie* (1788)

Honoré de Balzac, *Le Lys dans la vallée* (1835–36)

Honoré de Balzac, *Études de moeurs* (1844)

Stendhal, *Le Rouge et le Noir* (1830)

Honoré de Balzac, *La Physiologie du marriage* (1829)

Honoré de Balzac, *Le Voleur* (1830)

[Madame de La Fayette], La Princesse de Clèves (1678)

Honoré de Balzac, *Eugénie Grandet* (1833)

Gustave Flaubert, *Madame Bovary* (1857)

Victor Hugo, *Les Misérables* (1862)

Émile Zola, *La Faute de l'abbé Mouret* (1875)

Émile Zola, "*Un Bain,*" in *Contes à Ninon* (1864)

Émile Zola, *La Fortune des Rougon* (1871)

Émile Zola, *La Conquête de Plassans* (1874)

Émile Zola, *Une Page d'amour* (1878)

Émile Zola, *Le Rêve* (1888)

Émile Zola, *L'Oeuvre* (1886)

Émile Zola, *L'Assommoir* (1877)

Émile Zola, *La Curée* (1872)

Guy de Maupassant, *La Serre* (1883)

Guy de Maupassant, *Un Cas de divorce* (1886)

MARCEL PROUST, OR THE GARDEN RE-CREATED

Marcel Proust, *À la recherche du temps perdu* (1909-1922)

Du côté de chez Swann (1913)

Un Amour de Swann (1913)

Du côté des Guermantes (1921-22)

Marcel Proust, *Contre Sainte-Beuve* (1954)

Marcel Proust, *Jean Santeuil* (1895)

Marcel Proust, *Le Temps retrouvé* (1927)

Reynaldo Hahn, in *Hommage à Marcel Proust* (1923)

Jacques de Lacretelle, in *Hommage à Marcel Proust (1923)*

Marcel Proust, *L'Indifférent* (1896)

ANDRÉ GIDE, LOVER OF GARDENS

André Gide, *Journal* (1887-1925; 1926-1950)

Albert Camus, "Rencontres avec André Gide," in *l'Hommage de la N.R.F* (November 1951)

André Gide, *L'Immoraliste* (1902)

André Gide, *La Porte étroite* (1909)

André Gide, *Si le grain ne meurt* (1926)

André Gide, *Les Faux-Monnayeurs* (1925)

André Gide, *Les Nouvelles Nourritures* (1935)

André Gide, *Les Nourritures terrestres* (1897)

THE THOUSAND AND ONE GARDENS OF COLETTE

Colette, *La Naissance du jour* (1928)

Colette, *La Femme cachée* (1924)

Colette, *Trois, six, neuf* (1944)

Colette, *La Retraite sentimentale* (1907)

Colette, *La Maison de Claudine* (1922)

Colette, *Sido* (1929)

Colette, *"La Treille muscate"* (1932)

Colette, *Prisons et paradis* (1932, 1935)

Colette, *Pour un herbier* (1948)

Colette, *Les Vrilles de la vigne* (1908)

Colette, *La Vagabonde* (1911)

Colette, *De ma fenêtre* (1942)

Simone de Beauvoir, *La Force des choses* (1963)

JEAN-PAUL AND SIMONE IN THE JARDIN DU LUXEMBOURG

Simone de Beauvoir, *Mémoires d'une jeune fille rangée* (1958)

Simone de Beauvoir, *Tout compte fait* (1972)

Jean-Paul Sartre, *Les Mots* (1963)

Jean-Paul Sartre, *Entretiens* (c. 1970s)

Jean-Paul Sartre, *La Nausée* (1938)

Gaston Bachelard, *La Terre et les rêveries du repos* (1946)

Jean-Paul Sartre, *L'Enfance d'un chef* (1939)

Simone de Beauvoir, *La Force de l'âge* (1960)

ENTIRE DAYS IN THE PARK WITH MARGUERITE DURAS

Marguerite Duras, *Un Parc de roman*

Marguerite Duras, *La Famille Taneran* (1943)

Marguerite Duras, *Les Impudents* (1992)

Marguerite Duras, *La Vie tranquille* (1944)

Marguerite Duras, *Barrage contre le Pacifique* (1950)

Marguerite Duras, *L'Amant* (1984)

Marguerite Duras, *L'Homme atlantique* (1982)

Marguerite Duras, *Écrire* (1993)

Marguerite Duras, *Détruire dit-elle* (1969)

Marguerite Duras, *India Song* (1973)

Marguerite Duras, *Nathalie Granger* (1973)

Marguerite Duras, *Jaune le soleil* (1972)

Marguerite Duras, *Le Ravissement de Lol V. Stein* (1964)

Marguerite Duras, *Le Vice-Consul* (1965)

THE INVISIBLE GARDENS OF PATRICK MODIANO

Patrick Modiano, *Pour que tu ne te perdes pas dans le quartier* (2014)

Patrick Modiano, *La Place de l'Étoile* (1968)

Patrick Modiano, *Villa triste* (1975)

Patrick Modiano, *Dora Bruder* (1997)

Patrick Modiano, *Rue des boutiques obscures* (1978)

Patrick Modiano, *L'Herbe de nuits* (2012)

Patrick Modiano, *Dans le café de la jeunesse perdue* (2007)

Patrick Modiano, *Un pedigree* (2005)

Patrick Modiano, *Remise de peine* (1988)

Patrick Modiano, *Chien de printemps* (1993)

CHRISTIAN BOBIN, GARDENER IN PARADISE

Christian Bobin, *L'Inespérée* (1994)

Christian Bobin, *Le Très-Bas* (1992)

Christian Bobin, *Autoportrait au radiateur* (1997)

Christian Bobin, *La Grande Vie* (2014)

Christian Bobin, *Une bibliothèque de nuages* (2006)

Christian Bobin, *Ressusciter* (2001)

Christian Bobin, *La Lumière du monde* (2001)

Christian Bobin, *La Dame blanche* (2007)

Christian Bobin, *La Grande Vie* (2015)

Christian Bobin, *Les Ruines du ciel* (2009)

Christian Bobin, *L'Homme-Joie* (2012)

BIBLIOGRAPHY

Baraton, Alain. *Dictionnaire amoureux des jardins*. Paris: Plon, 2012.

Baridon, Michel. *Les Jardins: Paysagistes, jardins, poètes*. Paris: Robert Laffont, 1998.

Bénetières, Marie-Hélène. *Jardins, vocabulaire typologique et technique*. Paris: Éditions du Patrimoine, 2000.

Bernard-Griffiths, Simone, and Marie-Cécile Levet, eds. *Fleurs et jardins dans l'œuvre de George Sand*. Centre de recherches révolutionnaires et romantiques. Clermont-Ferrand: Presses universitaires Blaise-Pascal de Clermont-Ferrand, 2004.

Bloch-Dano, Évelyne. *La Fabuleuse Histoire des légumes*. Paris: Grasset, 2008. Translated by Teresa Lavender Fagan as *Vegetables: A Biography*. Chicago: University of Chicago Press, 2012.

Bouchenot-Déchin, Patricia. *André Le Nôtre*. Paris: Fayard, 2013.

Bourgoing, Catherine de, ed. *Jardins romantiques français: Du jardin des Lumières au parc romantique*. Exhibition catalogue. Paris: Paris musées, 2011.

Cahiers, Colette. No. 14, "Habitants de Saint-Tropez." Rennes: Presses universitaires de Rennes, 1992.

Chamblas-Ploton, Mic. *Les Jardins d'André Gide*. Paris: Éditions du Chêne, 1998.

Chansigaud, Valérie. *Une histoire des fleurs: Entre nature et culture*. Paris: Delachaux et Niestlé, 2014.

Charageat, Marguerite. *L'Art des jardins*. Paris: Presses universitaires de France, 1962.

Clément Gilles. *Une brève histoire du jardin*. Paris: Jean-Claude Béhar, 2012.

———. *Éloge des vagabondes: Herbes, arbres et fleurs à la conquête du monde*. Paris: NiL Éditions, 2002.

———. *La Sagesse du jardinier*. Paris: Jean-Claude Béhar, 2012.

———. *Traité succinct de l'art involontaire*. Paris: Sense & Tonka, 2014.

Colette, Florence, and Denise Péricard-Méa, eds. *Le Temps des jardins*. Seine-et-Marne: Côté jardin, 1992.

Conan, Michel. *L'Art des jardins*. Paris: Hazan, 1997.

Descola, Philippe. *Les Formes du paysage*. Cours d'anthropologie de la nature du Collège de France. www.college-de-France.fr.

Foucault, Michel. "Des Espaces autres." *Architecture, Mouvement, Continuité*, no. 5 (October 1984): 46–49. Translated by Jay Miskowiec as "Of Other Spaces: Utopias and Heterotopias," *Diacritics* 16, no. 1 (Spring 1986): 22–27.

Grimal, Pierre. "L'art des jardins." In *Rome et l'Amour*. Paris: Robert Laffont, 2007.

———. *Les Jardins romains*. Paris: Fayard, 1984.

Hirschfeld, C. C. L. *Theory of Garden Art*. Edited and translated by Linda B. Parshall. Philadelphia: University of Pennsylvania Press, 2001.

Hunt, John Dixon. *L'Art du jardin et son histoire*. Paris: Odile Jacob, 1996.

Impelluso, Lucia. *Jardins, potagers et labyrinthes*. Translated from the Italian by Jacques Bonnet. Paris: Hazan, 2005.

Le Dantec, Jean-Pierre. *Le Sauvage et le Régulier: Art des jardins au xxᵉ siècle*. Le Moniteur, 2002.

Lefébure, Amaury, and Christophe Pincemaille. *Joséphine, La passion des fleurs et des oiseaux*. Exhibition catalogue. Musée national des châteaux de Malmaison et Bois-Préau, 2014.

Legrain, Michel. *Guide du paradis*. Paris: Armand Colin, 2010.

Ligne, Charles-Joseph de. *Coup d'œil sur Belœil*, 1781.

Louis XIV. *Manière de montrer les jardins de Versailles*. Edited by Simone Hoog. Paris: Réunion des musées nationaux, 1982.

Meiller, Daniel, and Paul Vannier. *Le Grand Livre des fruits et légumes*. Paris: La Manufacture, 1991.

Moreau, Jean-Luc. *Le Paris de Jean-Paul Sartre et Simone de Beauvoir*. Paris: Éditions du Chêne, 2001.

Mosser, Monique. *Histoire des jardins de la Renaissance à nos jours*. Paris: Flammarion, 2002.

Orsenna, Erik. *Portrait d'un homme heureux*. Paris: Gallimard, "Folio," 2002.

Paris-Guide par les principaux écrivains et artistes de France. Part 2. "La Vie," by A. Lacroix. Paris: Verboeckhaven et Cie, 1867.

Peylet, Gérard, ed. "Les Mythologies du jardin de l'Antiquité à la fin du XIXe siècle." *Eidôlon*. Bordeaux: Presses universitaires de Bourdeaux, 2006.

Quellier, Florent. *Histoire du jardin potager*. Paris: Armand Colin, 2012.

Racine, Michel. *Créatures de jardins en France de la Renaissance au XXIe siècle*. 2 vols. Arles: Actes Sud/ENSP, 2001-2.

Sand, Christiane, and Gilles Clément. *Le Jardin romantique de George Sand*. Paris: Albin Michel, 1995.

Sicotte, Geneviève. *Le Jardin dans la littérature fin de siècle ou quand un motif narratif devient un objet esthétique*. http://www.projectsdepaysage.fr.

Taquet, Philippe. *Les Bonnes Feuilles du jardin des plantes de Jean-Jacques Rousseau à Claude Simon*, an anthology. Paris: Muséum national d'histoire naturelle, 2013.

Vanautgaerden, Alexandre. *Un jardin philosophique*. Brussels: La Lettre volée à la Maison d'Erasme, 2001.

Zard, Philippe. *L'Arbre et le Philosophe: Du platane de Barrès au marronnier de Sartre*. http://www.revue-silene.com/images/30/extrait_133.pdf.

List of libraries and archives holding collections on gardens: http://www.culture.gouv.fr/nav/index-dt.html.

Website of the media library of the Société nationale d'horticulture de France: www.snhf.org/mediatheque.